DEDICATION

*To Cami, who loves fishes; Uncle Kevin, who loves the water;
and to Uncle Brett and Aunt Sonya, who understand the ocean.*

What kind of sharks
go to heaven when
they die?

Angel sharks!

ACKNOWLEDGMENTS

To Faith, Jana, and Wanda for all of their help.

What part of a shark
weighs the most?

The scales!

Contents

The EVERYTHING KIDS' Sharks Book

Introduction

Have you ever wondered what it would be like to live in the ocean? Have you ever imagined what it must be like to swim around all day long, eating whatever you want, whenever you want, or being able to scare somebody simply by opening your mouth? Well, then *The Everything® Kids' Sharks Book* is for you! This fun-filled book will let you see the world through the eyes of a shark—a wet and wild world.

Take a journey down to the deepest part of the ocean, travel back to the beginning of time, visit an aquarium, become a fossil hunter, and see what it's like to be a famous "movie star." But your adventures won't stop there. You can learn how to "hide" like a shark, float like a shark, or even play cards like one. Maybe your favorite part of this book will be making an ocean you can eat or challenging your friends to a survival competition. Or maybe the thing you like doing the most will be the experiments or the sand art. Either way, you'll discover why some people think sharks are monsters while others think they are man's best friend.

In between the covers of this book, you'll find out how sharks smell trouble and how they see things very differently from us. You will also learn the "shocking" truth about the way sharks find their food, how they travel throughout the ocean, and where they raise their families. There are hours of fun games and puzzles just waiting inside this book for you.

So, when does the adventure start? Right now! Get your swimsuit and goggles ready because you're probably going to get wet. Then pack your towels, grab your sand shovel, and prepare to dig into this book. Don't forget to invite your family and friends.

There's plenty of fun to go around for everyone—here is your chance to get everyone to try eating edible sand, searching for shark's teeth, or just getting them to take a day off and go to the beach. But remember to warn your friends and family, this book is about *sharks,* you know. So, *everyone out of the water!* It's time to start reading!

First shark: Say, are you still dating that terrific-looking lobster?

Second shark: No, he was too shellfish!

Chapter 1

An Ancient, Enormous Aquarium

The Ocean, the First Aquarium

Imagine the world as a very large fishbowl, with only one piece of land in it—much like an island. Way back in the beginning this is how it was. Apart from that one giant piece of land, everything else in the world at that time was water. On land was the fresh water we know as rivers and lakes, but most of the water was in the form of an enormous ocean stretching off in all directions.

Many scientists believe that in the *very* beginning of time, the earth was dry. They also think that our planet was covered with volcanoes. As the volcanoes began to erupt, clouds formed and rain poured down everywhere, making the body of water that became the first ocean. As the water covered the salty ground, the first salt water was made.

One thing all sharks have in common is that they need water, lots and lots of water that is filled with salt, in order to live. So you might think that in the beginning of time there were tons of sharks and fish swimming around in this massive body of water. Actually, all that existed in the water were creatures too small to see. It would take a long time, a billion years or so, before small fish, amphibians, and finally the sharks could be found.

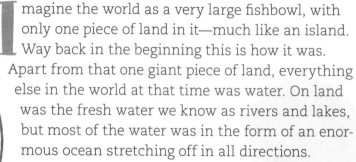

Words to Know

aquarium:
An *aquarium* is a container of fresh or salt water where fish and other animals can live. Aquariums can be as small as a fish bowl or as large as a building.

Solving the Puzzle

"So," you might be wondering, "how do we know all of this? If there were no people there at the time, how can we be sure what really lived here?" The only way we can guess is through the study of geology. *Geologists* are people who study the rocks of the earth for clues to the mystery of our past. They find the pieces to this puzzle hidden deep in our earth's crust, in the images captured in stones from the ocean's floor. These pieces of stone have washed ashore, or they might have moved inland when the earth changed from one island to become the separated lands and water that we know today. Although people were not here to see the world as it was changing, the sharks and dinosaurs were. Sharks were one of the first things on our planet. During the great changes on the planet many land animals vanished, but the sharks were lucky because they were protected in their underwater world.

Let's Go to the Beach

Why not take a day and go to the beach? If you don't have an ocean close by, how about hunting for treasure along the banks of a river or the shore of a lake? There are all kinds of treasures and clues to be found near the water, like rocks and footprints. You might even find some small frogs, fish, or animals. But don't forget to bring along your family, some lunch, and a few containers for catching and carrying your creatures. Just remember to let them go before you head home, because most fish and animals require a very special habitat to survive.

Fossilized Fish

Do you like hunting for treasure? The ocean hides treasures of all kinds. Once in a while it even sends a few of its treasures ashore. All you have to do is walk along the beach in the morning to find beautiful shells, starfish, and clams, among other things. If you're lucky, you may even find a triangle-shaped prize that once belonged in the mouth of a shark. These black, blue, or sometimes white pointed objects

Ocean Cake

To make an ocean cake, all you need is a box of white cake mix. Follow the directions for mixing it up, then add a few drops of blue food coloring to the batter. Pour it into a pan, and have your parents bake it. Once the cake is cool, you can hide a few gummy sharks down in the cake and then frost it with blue-colored whipped topping.

What am I?

To hear my name you might think of Moby Dick. But my spots always give me away. Don't let my size fool you. I may be very large, but the food I crave is very small. **What am I?**

Whale shark

 3

Try This

A Bone to Pick

If sharks' teeth can change colors, can bones? Ask your local butcher if he has any extra bones he could give you. (Ham bones work well for this experiment.) Then have one of your parents boil the bone and let it cool. Now place the cool bone in a jar with water and a few drops of blue food coloring. Cover the jar. Try to guess what will happen to the bone. Were you right?

Words to Know

fossil:

A *fossil* is a solidified object produced by an organism that has been perfectly preserved in rock or stone. Fossils have taught us a lot about the sharks of the past.

are sharks' teeth. Treasure seekers just like you have collected sharks' teeth for millions of years. If you find a white one, it is not very old. But if you find a blue or black one, it is much older and has become a fossil. A shark's teeth change in color by taking in the minerals and other materials from the area around them.

It takes many years to form a fossil. If a plant, animal, or shark dies and its remains stay in the same place, covered in sand, it can become a fossil. Minerals from the water fill the plant or animal. As the remains decay, water and minerals fill the empty space where the shark, plant, or animal once was. As the sand and minerals harden in the space, they create an image of the object that was there. Fossils have also helped us to learn about changes in the Earth's weather, land, and water.

The majority of shark fossils show only their teeth. But, the search went on over the years, and eventually a fossil was found that showed a shark's teeth, skin, and muscles. Before this fossil was found, humans could only guess what the ancient sharks might have looked like. Newer fossils have helped us to see that long ago, some sharks had noses that were up towards the top of their heads and mouths that were in the front of their face—like yours!

Sometimes the marks from the shark's teeth on another animal's fossilized bones are the only proof we have that the shark was there! Did you know that the tooth marks from each type of shark are different? This is the way that we can tell which sharks were living at a certain time.

Clues from the Past

Do you remember the last thing you had to eat? How about what you had for lunch yesterday? Some fossils have been found that even show what a shark ate for its last lunch!

Bigger Than Big

The tremendous shark megalodon lived about 25 million years ago. It is thought to have been 50 feet long, or longer! No one has ever found a fossil of a complete megalodon, but they have found many fossils of one particular part of this ancient giant. Follow the directions below to see what the scientific name MEGALODON means, and you will find a description of the fossils that have been found.

Write the name MEGALODON _____

Move the G to the beginning _____

Move the A to second place _____

Move the N to third place _____

Move the O to the end _____

Delete MEL _____

Change D to T _____

Add I between G and A _____

Double the T _____

Add TH to the end _____

Watch Out!
If this scuba diver is 6 feet tall, how big is the megalodon that is sneaking up on him?

These fossils or images created from rock have recorded our planet's history in a perfect form that seems to last forever. Fossils can tell us a lot about how the earth and the animals appeared long ago. Even if you live far from the sea, you can still have fun looking for fossils. Many fossils have been found inland literally hundreds of miles from the nearest shorelines.

If you want to try and find a few fossils of your own, you can look in a pile of decorative rocks or gravel. Almost anything can be fossilized: ferns, trees, plants, and animals, even dinosaurs. Many of the things we know today about the past came from these stones containing history.

Living Fossils

Fossils have helped us to "take a look" into the past. Some modern sharks have been called "living fossils" because they look almost identical to the sharks that used to swim in the same ocean millions of years ago. To see what an early shark looked like, all you have to do is find a picture of one of these "living fossils," like the hagfish or the lamprey.

When you think of a shark, what do you think of first? Most people would answer, "the shark's jaws." Can you imagine a shark without a jaw or not having all those teeth? The hagfish and lamprey, which are descendants of the first fish families, have a mouth, but strangely they have no jaws. These hagfish and lampreys have to use suction rather than teeth to hang on to their prey. The spiny dogfish that lives in the ocean today still has the same horn or spine-like weapon in front of its fin—and like its ancestors, the dogfish is still prepared to use it.

Words to Know

evolved:

When something has *evolved,* it means that it has changed. As cats and dogs have evolved, or changed, over many, many years, they have become smaller. Humans have grown taller, and our brains are getting larger. Some sharks have evolved to allow them to adjust to the changes in their ocean home.

Some sharks have changed and evolved over the years—they eventually grew jaws, lost some of their gills, or changed their form completely. Yet other members of the shark family have hardly changed or evolved at all. One mystery of the sharks that remains to be solved is how some sharks have never changed.

A Different World

Because we live on the land, the ocean is like a different world to us. For example, the weight of the ocean is a lot heavier than the weight of air. Air presses down on you each day at a pressure close to twenty pounds, which is the same as walking around all day with two bags of sugar on your

What am I?

If you were ever sick, you might think I could help you. Some may say I am a more caring shark. I am the familiar brown-colored shark you see at a lot of aquariums. **What am I?**

Nurse shark

Family Reunion

Do the following equation and you'll find out how many shark species scientists know about . . . at the moment!

Start with the number of gills you see here...

Multiply by the number of eyes the hammerhead has...

Multiply by the number of dorsal fins on the Port Jackson...

Subtract the total number of fins on the whaler...

Multiply by the number of pilot fish by the sand shark!

Port Jackson

sand

whaler

hammerhead

Shrinking Sharks

You can make your own shark's teeth or shark charms by using the clear lid from a birthday cake or deli tray you bought at the store. With your parents' help, color and cut out the teeth or sharks from this plastic. Punch a hole to string them on later. Bake them for a few minutes at 350 degrees.

What am I?

If you were thirsty and you heard my name, you might be tempted to squeeze me. But be careful, as other sharks may come to my "ade." My bright yellow color allows me to stand out in a crowd.

What am I?

Lemon shark

shoulders. Every inch of your body feels this weight each day. No wonder you feel tired at night! Towards the bottom of the ocean, the water's pressure is a thousand times greater than that. So if you were a shark trying to breathe at the bottom of the ocean, it would be sort of the same as you trying to breathe with an elephant sitting on you! (This doesn't bother the sharks, of course—they have always lived underwater and are used to it.)

Mystery of Lost Color

Other things are very different in the ocean, too. Color, as we know it, can only be seen in the first few feet below the surface of the ocean. The farther down in the water you go, the darker it gets, and the more the color changes until finally it disappears. How well do you see colors in the dark? For fun, invite someone to a color challenge. You and a friend or your brother or sister can test each other. All you need are a few different colored crayons and a room that you can make dark. Take turns trying out this test:

1. Have your partner hold the crayons up one by one for you to see, while the room still has light in it, so you can tell them the name of each color.
2. Try naming the colors again with a little less light in the room (make sure your partner mixes up the order to really test your eyes).
3. Try it one more time when the room is almost dark. What do you see?

Don't forget to give each person a turn to test his or her eyes!

Color isn't the only thing that disappears below the water; light is scarce as well. Many of the sharks that live in the very bottom of the oceans don't use their eyes much. No one is completely sure if they ever used them, or if these fish just evolved or changed because they no longer needed to see. Whatever the reason, the eyes of these bottom dwellers look quite different from the eyes of the creatures that live closer to the surface.

Temperature in the Ocean

Sharks spend twenty-four hours a day in the water. Some of the water is very cold, while other parts of the ocean are warmer. Most sharks migrate to warmer places each year, traveling thousands of miles. These sharks swim back to the colder waters to bear their young and find food.

Just like water, air can be hot or cold. When hot air from the land moves over the cold water, sometimes it turns the ocean water upside down, something like the way your stomach rolls over on the hills or loops of a roller coaster ride. When the water rolls over, it mixes up plankton from tiny plants and animals and brings them to the top of the water near the shore. Fish, large and small, follow the food. The plankton that surface don't remain at the top for long though. Once this cycle starts, they will travel distances of up to a mile each day to reach the top of the ocean for food, then return back down toward the bottom for safety.

Fish Families

If you were part of the bony fish family, you could be invited to the biggest family reunion on the planet. Your family has the largest variety of members around. The one relative you won't find there is a shark. Although they are fish, somehow sharks and their cousins, the rays and the skates, were overlooked when backbones were being handed out. This doesn't seem to bother them though.

Fun Fact

Bite Marks
Sharks will take a bite out of almost anything, even metal. One type of shark, which scientists thought had vanished millions of years ago, took a bite at a metal cable and left tooth marks that matched those from a 100-million-year-old fossil. Talk about leaving your mark behind!

Which One?

You might think it would be fun to take a ride on me. But because I don't have any spurs, you may have to bring your own along. I am one of the few creatures in the ocean that can swim standing up. Do you know which one I am?

   A. Walking fish
   B. Octopus
   C. Seahorse
   D. Jellyfish

C. Seahorse

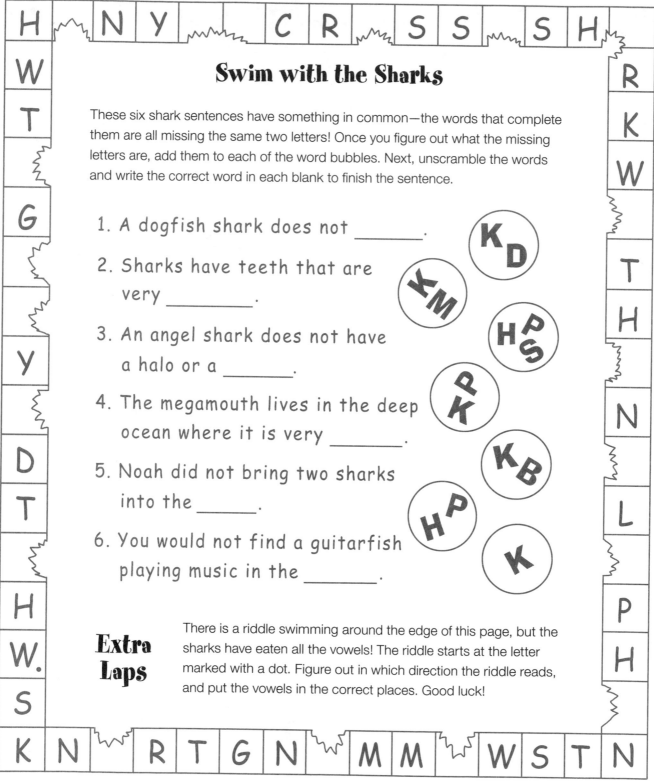

Swim with the Sharks

These six shark sentences have something in common—the words that complete them are all missing the same two letters! Once you figure out what the missing letters are, add them to each of the word bubbles. Next, unscramble the words and write the correct word in each blank to finish the sentence.

1. A dogfish shark does not _____.

2. Sharks have teeth that are very _____.

3. An angel shark does not have a halo or a _____.

4. The megamouth lives in the deep ocean where it is very _____.

5. Noah did not bring two sharks into the _____.

6. You would not find a guitarfish playing music in the _____.

Extra Laps

There is a riddle swimming around the edge of this page, but the sharks have eaten all the vowels! The riddle starts at the letter marked with a dot. Figure out in which direction the riddle reads, and put the vowels in the correct places. Good luck!

There's another thing that separates sharks from their other fish relatives—sharks don't make any sound. Other fish make all sorts of sounds, from shrieks to moans. But our silent friend the shark doesn't seem to want or need to communicate with anyone. Still, research has shown that sharks can be communicated with or taught. In "shark school," scientists have discovered that sharks can recognize different things such as shapes and colors. These shark students are rewarded with food if they swim to right place, which is marked with a special shape or color. If you want, you could test your friends' ability to learn. Try asking them a few shark trivia questions, like "Which shark has the biggest mouth?" and then reward them with a prize or treat.

Go Fish

Whoever decided to sort the fish into families had a lot of work to do. There are so many different kinds of fish, where would you start? How about with the sharks? For fun, you and your friends can sort them into your own groups. Follow these steps, and you're on your way:

1. Collect a few pictures of some sharks or fish from old magazines.
2. Get several pieces of paper to write your group names on, a marker, and a pair of scissors.
3. Sort your sharks by size, color, where they live, what they eat, or how they look.
4. After you've sorted them, cut each shark or fish into three equal parts. Mix the pictures up to create new creatures, or turn them face down and play a game of "Go Fish."

Try This

Edible Sand Art

If you want to try your hand at sand art you can eat, all you need are a few different colors of powdered gelatin. Take a clear jar and pour in layers of different colors until you almost reach the top. Now stick the handle of a spoon into the jar and pull it back up through the powder. Your gelatin "sand" will move and blend, creating a piece of art that is fun to look at and fun to taste. To taste your art just lick a spoon and stick it in the powder.

Which One?

Some people think I am too quiet or cold. Others think I should be baked. I'm happy just to lie around on the ocean floor. Do you know which one I am?

  A. Starfish
  B. Coral
  C. Lobster
  D. Clam

D. Clam

Fun Fact

Seven to Five

Fish families have been around for more than 400 million years. Some members of the first fish family can still be seen swimming in the ocean today. One way to tell how long a certain type of shark has been around is by counting its gills. The original types of sharks have six or seven sets of gills. Newer types have only five.

Mixing It All Up

Some of the members of the fish family appear to have gotten mixed up. The angel shark looks like a cross between a shark and a ray. This flat-bodied shark almost appears to have wings in place of its fins. But this shark soon proves it's more of a shark than an angel as it lies hidden on the ocean floor waiting for its prey. Another shark that looks like a mixture of two things is a sawshark, whose nose looks a lot like a saw you might find in a toolbox. This silly fish also looks like it's wearing a mustache.

The Name Game

Have you ever wondered how all the sharks got their names? All of the plants and animals on our planet belong to kingdoms or families. These kingdoms aren't like the ones with kings and queens; instead, they are the way scientists group things into categories. The name given to the shark family is "Selachian" because it means "shark-like" in Greek. After an animal is placed in a family, the members of the family are then divided into smaller groups, usually by their appearance or behavior. One of the ways sharks are grouped is by the size of their tails. Other ways include the number of dorsal fins that they have, the number of gills on their sides, what the shark likes to eat, or even its basic shape. The shark family contains more than 300 groups. Because new discoveries are made every day, the number of kinds of sharks constantly grows.

Chapter 2

On the Defense

 **Try This**

Look Mom, No Hands!

A great way to relate to a shark is to try this "no hands" relay. All you need is two lines, both with the same number of people. To start, the first person in each line places a grapefruit under his or her chin, passing it on to the next person's neck without letting either person touch the grapefruit with their hands. The first line to get its grapefruit to the end wins.

Survival of the Fittest

By now you have probably figured out that with all the big changes going on around the earth, the shark has had to be pretty tough. Sharks have also had to adapt to their environment. When you study really hard to get good grades, practice sports to perform well and win a game, or make an effort to be nice to people, you know what it's like to try your hardest to succeed and fit in with your classmates, teammates, and friends. Much like the shark, you work hard to make a place for yourself. You have to make choices and learn to adapt to your surroundings and the people in your world to succeed.

Gold Medal Sharks

If you decided to hold an Olympic contest tomorrow, the shark family would probably win most of the events. The blue shark is used to swimming very long distances because it travels thousands of miles each year to migrate, and it would probably win the swim marathon. The mako shark could win the medal for the fastest swimmer because it reaches speeds of around fifty miles an hour. The record for deep-sea diving would have to go to the megamouth shark, because it can swim thousands of feet down below the ocean's surface only to travel back all the way back up to the top again each night. The megamouth would probably win the title of strongest fish, too, since it is able to support thousands of pounds of water pressure on every inch of its body. Then there's the thresher shark, which uses its tail like

a hockey stick, and that would join the great white shark to make a prize-winning team for penguin volleyball, bouncing those poor little penguins way up in the air just for fun. The high-jumping contest would go to the basking shark, a shark that is as big as a house that spends its time jumping up out of the water trying to get rid of the parasites or pests that cling to it. Can you imagine being famous for trying to get someone or something to quit bugging you?

What's Bugging You?

Do mosquitoes or flies ever "bug you"? Some parasites not only bug sharks, but they can also hurt them. Some reef sharks have been seen waiting in line to have the insects removed from their bodies by a small type of fish known as a wrasse. These hungry little wrasse fish don't stop until the shark is completely clean. Other sharks, like the lemon and zebra sharks, have their own personal cleaners—fish called remoras that travel throughout the ocean with them.

One thing that is very different about the remoras is that they have a fin shaped like a suction cup. Once they are suctioned on to the shark, they ride along waiting for the left-over scraps that fall from the shark's mouth.

Luring with Light

Some of the parasites or pests that bug sharks are luminous, which means they can light up. The light attracts small fish down to the bottom, where eventually the sleeper shark eats them. If you were a shark trying to catch a fish down deep in the ocean, you might be able to do the same thing by putting a flashlight near your mouth, then you could quickly swallow up your victims as they swim toward the light.

Words to Know

parasite:
A *parasite* is something that feeds or lives off of something else without giving anything back to its host or food supply. For instance, lice are a parasite that feeds off sharks.

Fun Fact

Stiff Fins
A shark's pectoral fins are stiffer and harder to move than those of a bony fish. The shark uses these fins to steer and balance itself as it swims through the water.

Other sharks have been known to lure their lunches with lights that glow from their abdomen, like the lantern shark does. Maybe you have seen this type of luminous glow if you've ever snapped a glowstick (the kind you can use like a bright-colored light or wear around your neck like a necklace). A lantern shark's light starts to shine when two liquids mix inside its body, very much like a glow stick.

What's That Glowing?

Another way to see an example of this strange glow is to write a message on your hand with a fluorescent highlighter or marker and then hold it under a black light bulb. If you don't have a black light bulb, you can buy one at most hardware stores.

Several other things light up in the dark, too—like nightlights, for example. How many things can you list that "glow" in your home? Try writing down all the things that you can think of that light up at night to help you find your way around your house, after the lights are turned out. Then later when it gets dark, check to see how many things you had right and how many you missed. Can your family name all of them?

The Bigger They Are

Over the years, scientists have noticed that the bigger a shark is, the faster it can swim. They have also figured out that a shark's best chance for survival relies on being the fastest in its group. So how bad could it really be, to be a small, slow shark? Pretty bad—and to make things worse, sharks that are sometimes known as the top killers, such as the great white and mako, are warm-blooded. This allows

Words to Know

symbiosis:
When two animals help each other, like the shark and the remora, it is called *symbiosis*. Animals or sharks that have learned to live close by each other and work together have this relationship of symbiosis. When they help each other, both can exist.

Which One?

Should you ever try to keep an eye on me, be careful because I will be keeping two on you. But watch very closely, for if I turn you may not see me at all. Do you know which one I am?

   A. Flatfish
   B. Bat fish
   C. Sailfish
   D. Swordfish

A. Flatfish

them to move faster than their cold-blooded prey. So these small, cold-blooded sharks must stay in top condition so they can rely on their ability to hide and think fast.

One game you can do that relies on speed and listening closely is Red Light, Green Light. Only this time, try it in the swimming pool. You never know when the leader will yell "red light," signaling for you to stop. To play, all you need is a few friends or family members. Then someone is chosen to start the game as the "leader." When everyone is in a line and ready, the leader calls out "green light." Everyone swims as fast as they can toward the leader until they hear the words "red light," then the players start to dog-paddle, until they hear the words "green light" again. The first person to reach the leader becomes the new leader and the game starts all over again.

Camouflaged Creatures

You go to the seashore with your parents to search for a star-fish, and then you spy one just under some colorful rocks along the edge of the water. You reach down to grab it, but then the rocks start to move. Believe it or not, you have just found a wobbegong, the disguise artist from Down Under. Down under where, you ask? That's what some people call Australia, and that's where this giant-sized fish lure comes from. The skin around a wobbegong's mouth looks like seaweed, which tricks the fish that are swimming close by into trying to take a bite, only to have this sly shark eat them instead.

If you are walking along in the shallow water, and you feel the sand move beneath your feet, beware! It might be the tan-colored angel shark that

What am I?

I love to lay around all day long soaking up the sun. Because I am so big and appear from time to time off in the distance, some people actually thought I was a sea monster. **What am I?**

Basking shark

Color me in!

Where's Wobbegong?

The wobbegong is a bottom-dwelling shark. It blends in so well with the ocean floor that small fish will swim right up to it! Can you find the two wobbegongs lying on this coral reef?

See if you can also find the glove, needle and thread, sock, pennant, Santa hat, teacup, butterfly, pickle, paper clip, ice cream cone, snake, ghost, bunny, fried egg, and crown.

likes to bury itself under the sand and hide. Sharks come in all shapes and sizes, and they come in different patterns and colors too! You might wonder if you're on a safari when you hear of the leopard, tiger, and zebra sharks. Just like the animals on land that have the same names, these sharks use their patterns of color to protect themselves or to help them hunt. As these sharks get older, sometimes their stripes will change to spots, making it even harder to know their family name.

Now You See It

Many creatures use camouflage as a way to trick your brain into not seeing what is right before your eyes.

Have you walked through your yard and been surprised by a rabbit hiding under a bush? Baby fawns, with their speckled coats, blend so well into the brown colors of the trees that you may never see them until they show their bright white tails as they run away. Do you have any clothes that are covered with patches of brown and green? Clothes like this, often called "camos," are what some people wear when they are playing games like paint-ball or if they go hunting or fishing. What would you wear if you were trying to hide in the snow, night, forest, water, grass, or the sand?

Would you like to be able to change the color of your skin depending on whether you were going to be in the shade or the sun? What if your skin could change instantly to match a new landscape? One of the shark's favorite foods, the octopus, can do just that. Their skin is covered with cells that are like containers of paint. They can choose whatever color they want to be. Wouldn't it be nice if your bike could be like that? The only problem would be if you forgot and left it on the camouflage setting and then couldn't find it!

Words to Know

camouflage:
Some sharks use *camouflage* as a way to hide or conceal themselves from others. Their camouflage might be stripes, patches, spots, or colors. The camouflage helps them to blend in with their surroundings.

What's Your Name?
Some sharks have more than one name. The wobbegong shark is also called a carpet shark because of its shaggy appearance. It looks a lot like a rug you might find on your floor.

Which One?

You might expect to see me wearing a round, red nose, but instead you will probably find me hiding in amongst the anemones. Do you know which one I am?

A. Dogfish
B. Sucker
C. Clownfish

C. Clownfish

What am I?

Some believe I should be in a field instead of the ocean, with my tail that is shaped like a sickle. But I prefer to harvest fish with my tail rather than grain. **What am I?**

Thresher shark

A Color Change You *Don't* Want

Next time you pack to go to the beach, what will you pack? You probably thought of your flip-flops, swimsuit, and sunglasses right away, but did you remember your sunscreen? Without it, your skin will probably change color too! Although your skin doesn't change instantly, it can change color over a few hours. So, remember that even if you put sunscreen on when you first get there, if you want to keep from turning pink or red, it's best to reapply it after you've been in the water. Here are a few rules to keep you from looking like a lobster:

- In the middle of the day, when the sun is strongest, do not play on the beach for more than a few hours.
- Spend some of the time sitting in the shade.
- Cover yourself with a white shirt.
- Don't forget to wear a visor or a hat.

Try an experiment. Wear a black T-shirt out in the direct sunlight. Then try wearing other, different colors. Did you feel cooler when you were wearing the white shirt?

Tag, You're It!

Playing a game of tag at the beach could be fun. All you need are a couple of people and a few simple rules. Try to pick an area of the beach where you won't bother any other people, and then start making a large circle in the sand with your feet. When your circle is completed, make lines straight through the middle as though you were cutting pieces of pie. Gather your friends or family and decide who is going to be the "shark," then start running along the lines that you have drawn in the sand. The first fish that is caught by the "shark" now becomes the new "shark," and you start all over again.

The Great Escape

Are you afraid of anything? Some people are afraid of heights, while other people fear things like mice or spiders. Almost everyone has something they don't like to be around, but do you know why most people are afraid of the water? Sharks, of course! Have you ever wondered what sharks fear? They fear other, bigger sharks. One reason may be that they know that the big sharks can swallow them without taking a bite! Even the great white and the bull shark are said to fear the killer whales, which seem to be the only creatures in the ocean with no enemies to fear.

Size can be important. Have you ever heard the term "pecking order"? Some families have one, and most chickens

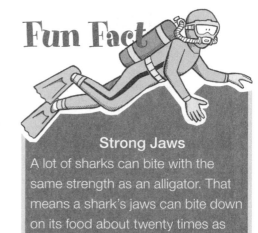

Fun Fact

Strong Jaws
A lot of sharks can bite with the same strength as an alligator. That means a shark's jaws can bite down on its food about twenty times as hard as yours can.

How Many School Buses Equal One Whale Shark?

The whale shark is the biggest fish in the ocean, weighing up to 15 tons! But how big is that really? Use the information below to see how much a whale shark weighs in more familiar terms.

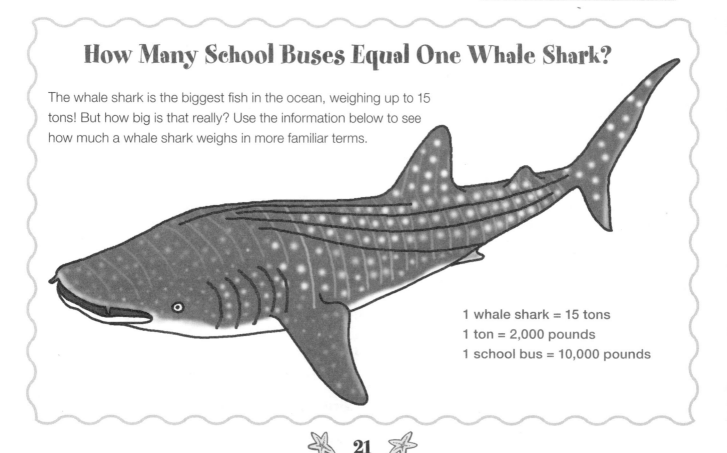

1 whale shark = 15 tons
1 ton = 2,000 pounds
1 school bus = 10,000 pounds

What am I?

When people talk about me, they say I am "great." Unfortunately, seals don't like me very much because I like to eat them. I am the most aggressive and dangerous of all of the sharks.

What am I?

Great white shark

seem to know what it means. For chickens, a pecking order means that they will only let certain chickens crowd ahead of them while they're in line, waiting for food. The rest have to wait their turn, or they get pecked. Ouch! Smaller sharks also have to learn to wait, although sometimes not too patiently, while the bigger sharks eat all they want from their meal. And although you might think only the smaller sharks fear the bigger sharks, it's not always true. Even some types of larger sharks seem to fear certain other shark families, so they also have to wait for their turn.

Simon Says

Have you ever played Simon Says with a bunch of your friends? Just like the sharks or chickens, you have to wait for

Let's Play

Use the decoder to figure out this riddle:

What's a shark's favorite game?

LET'S PLAY!

Let's not!

smack, yummy, gulp, urp, urp, slurp, yummy

yum, crunch, munch

urp, munch, gulp, gurgle, munch, crack

A = gulp	E = munch	L = urp	R = crack	T = yum
D = gurgle	H = crunch	O = slurp	S = smack	W = yummy

the person who is chosen to be Simon to tell you when you can "hop on your tail," "swim using only one fin," or "dog-paddle." The important thing to remember is to listen for the words "Simon says"—if Simon just calls out "move your fins" without saying "Simon says" first, and you move your fins anyway, you're out. The person who is Simon keeps calling out things to do until only one player is left, and then that player becomes the new Simon.

Fear Not

Sharks aren't just afraid of other sharks; they can also be scared of dolphins. Would you think those cute little playful dolphins could ever frighten a shark? They not only scare them; dolphins have been known to keep butting their heads against a shark's side until the shark is dead! Why would a shark with a name like the cookie-cutter make whales, dolphins, or other sharks worried? Especially since they're less than two feet long? It's not because they are killers. What the other animals don't like is how a cookie-cutter will swim up to their sides, grab onto them and bite down, then spin themselves around until they leave a small hole in their body.

The shark's greatest enemy seems to be humans. When a person enters the shark's neighborhood or area, the sharks usually try to give a warning so that he or she will leave. If you saw a mako shark swimming toward you, making a figure eight like an Olympic skater, you might think you had nothing to fear—right until it opened its mouth filled with teeth that are as big as a grown man's fingers! The gray reef shark prefers to hunch its back like an angry cat, scrunch up its nose, and push its pectoral fins downward as though it is putting on its brakes to let you know that it means business.

Most sharks have their own way to threaten you before they attack. If you continue to approach them, they further

Now That's a Big Fish!
The biggest fish of all is a shark known as the whale shark. This shark is so big it could barely turn around in an aquarium the size of your house.

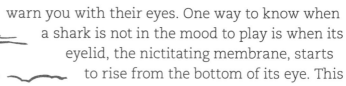
warn you with their eyes. One way to know when a shark is not in the mood to play is when its eyelid, the nictitating membrane, starts to rise from the bottom of its eye. This is the shark's way of letting you know there may be a fight. The nictitating membrane protects the shark's eyes so its victim can't damage them. These membranes work like the wipers on your car's windshield. They clean the shark's eyes as they pass over them.

Some people think that it's important to "Look them right in the eye when you talk to them," but that isn't always a good idea. Looking a person or animal in the eye can also mean you're looking for a fight. Making eye contact with a shark or any other wild animal is never a good plan.

Don't Go in the Water!

All those scary movies are right in one respect. If you see fins moving around on the surface of the ocean, don't go in the water! There aren't enough man-eaters to fill a Ten Most Wanted list for sharks, but any shark can be dangerous. Some are top killers, like the bull, tiger, and great white, but even these sharks usually don't set out to kill humans. If you could get the shark's side of the story, you'd see that a lot of shark attacks are accidents. If you are aware of the danger from sharks and know some of the things you can do to prevent an attack, it will be better for you *and* the sharks. If you see a sign posted on the beach that says "Beware of the

Words to Know

dorsal fin:
A *dorsal fin* is the fin that sits on the back of a shark or fish. The size and shape of these fins vary greatly from shark to shark.

Sharks," your family will know that this is a warning that must be obeyed.

Stay Out!

Sometimes you probably wish you could post a sign like this in your room whenever you want to have some time by yourself. You could always ask an adult in your family to help you make the sign and hang it on your door. One thing you could do is use a blackboard or magic slate. That way you could leave other messages for your family or use it as an ongoing game site. You could take turns and play tic-tac-toe, finish the word, or hangman each time you or anyone else went by your door.

If you have ever read the story *Goldilocks and the Three Bears,* you know that even though the little girl went into the bear's house and ate their food and broke their furniture, the bears still didn't hurt her. Any time you go to the beach or enter the shark's home, the ocean, there are a few rules you should know, so that you won't be harmed, either.

You might think it would be a good idea to take your dog along to the beach so he could enjoy the water. All that splashing might make a shark think a hurt or distressed animal is in the water, and to a shark that means it is time to eat! If you're riding a surfboard, the shark might think you look like a turtle, seal, or dolphin. The only thing the shark can see is the surfboard's outline, which does look a lot like a dolphin or turtle. If it is warm enough for you to swim in the water, it's warm enough for the sharks, too. But this doesn't mean sharks don't live or swim in cold water—sharks are found almost everywhere. Many bull sharks are at home in some lakes and have even been seen swimming in some big rivers. Imagine the shock of going to the river and seeing a dorsal fin traveling upstream?

Floating Fins

You can make your own floating shark fins using two disposable plastic plates or deli containers. The first plate is your base, and the second one is cut out to be your shark's fin. Make a fold at the bottom of the fin, then staple or tape the fin on the plate. You can float your fin in the pool and use it as a ring toss or target.

What am I?

You may be able to guess my name by my stripes, unless I am older and I have outgrown them. Like my namesake, I love to eat meat. **What am I?**

Tiger shark

The sandbar shark, which gets its name from swimming over the sand, may even be carried up onto the land by the ocean waves. Spotted epaulette sharks use their fins like little feet, so if they get trapped on shore, all they have to do is walk back into the water!

Shark Safety

You should always take an adult with you if you want to go into the water. You might think that swimming when the sun is coming up or going down would be the best time of the day because you wouldn't get sunburned. Unfortunately, that's when the shark's food is moving around in the water and so are they, so this is a time to be extra careful. Another thing that attracts sharks is bright jewelry. When they see something shimmering on your neck or arm in the sunlight, they think they are seeing fish scales. Take your jewelry off before you swim so those sharks don't think you are a fish!

It's important to remember that sharks, like all wild creatures, don't usually bother you unless you bother them. If you follow the rules of shark safety, the odds are pretty good that you will never meet up with one.

Color me in!

Chapter 3

Feeding Frenzy

Let's Eat

Have you ever gone to a family reunion? Sometimes people go home from these parties with an upset stomach. If this ever happened to you, your family might have thought it was due to all the excitement of seeing and meeting all those new people—when actually it was all the food you ate. Everyone kept saying, "Try some of this." It was all so good that you couldn't stop eating until it was time to go home. Seeing a large group of their family and the thought of eating large amounts of food can also influence sharks. No longer willing to wait their turn, they may even nip or bite a few of their own family members!

Sharks aren't the only type of fish that have feeding frenzies. Have you ever thrown fish food to giant goldfish in the pond at a park or zoo? You probably saw them get pretty excited about that food, too. They don't actually eat each other, but there sure is a lot of shoving and pushing around.

What's on the Menu?

In the ocean, the smallest creatures are the main source of food for the biggest of the fish. The original source of all the food in the ocean is the sun. Solar energy is needed to make all the tiny plants grow, and then the tiny animals feed upon them. Many of these organisms are too small to be seen without using a microscope. Others are baby lobsters, eels, starfish, and other meat-eaters that will soon be eating next year's crop of plankton.

Try This

Let's Go to the Movies

For fun, how about checking out a movie about sharks from your library or video store? It's an easy way to visit the ocean and a fun way to learn even more about sharks and other creatures from the deep. You might also want to try one on submarines or sea monsters. Just don't forget the popcorn!

This pattern of living things eating other living things is called a food chain, but some people call it a food web.

The term "food chain" makes you think that only one type of animal will eat a certain animal and that each eater will be bigger than the animal it eats. This would make you think that predators and their victims are always linked together. On the other hand, a "food web" describes what really happens! Most animals in the ocean, and especially the sharks, will eat lots of different things, even their own children. Sharks come back to the same areas every year to chase the schools of fish that they know will appear when the plankton are coming to the top of the water. Large animals, like the giant octopus, can be overcome by packs of small sharks. Even though they are the top predators in the ocean, sharks are an important part of the food web, since they help keep the ocean's population in balance.

Words to Know

feeding frenzy:
Sharks have been known to go into what is called a *feeding frenzy* if they get overly excited when they are hungry and want to eat. In their frenzy, these sharks may even take a bite out of each other.

Favorite Foods

Some of a shark's favorite foods are seals, swordfish, stingrays, dolphins, and, as we've mentioned before, other sharks. What are your favorite foods? At your next family reunion, picnic, or at mealtime at home, take a poll of what your family's favorite foods are. You might be surprised at the answers.

One way to learn your family's likes and dislikes might be to help them plan a few menus. Then you can help shop for the groceries or share in the fun of making a meal using your new menu ideas.

Open Wide!

Do you or any member of your family have what might be described as a mouth of enormous size? One way to check

Which One?

You might expect me to come out at night. Or maybe you think I am famous. Either way I usually have a point to make. Do you know which one I am?

  A. Lantern fish
  B. Starfish
  C. Lamprey
  D. Flame tetra

B. Starfish

Color me in!

this out is to make triple-decker sandwiches. There is no limit to what can go into these sandwiches. Just follow these simple steps:

1. Start with three slices of any type of bread.
2. Ask people if they want their bread toasted.
3. Provide them with a variety of sandwich meats like ham, turkey, chicken, or beef.
4. Most people like cheese, so give them a variety to choose from.
5. Be really daring and offer sardines or anchovies.
6. Then it's time for them to pile on the vegetables and dressing.

What you may find out is that, like the shark, you would need jaws that aren't fastened to your skull to fit a meal that big into your mouth. Sharks' teeth act sort of like a jack-in-the-box; when a shark opens its mouth, its teeth leap out at whatever the shark is trying to bite. The jaws can stretch very far apart so it can take a really big bite!

Most of the time a shark will sniff its food before it eats it. Do you ever do that? You would think with all that sniffing, a shark would know the difference between a man, a seal, or a fish. But when it is chasing all those other fish right below the surface of the water, it might go into one of those feeding frenzies and eat anything that it sees! Sharks have been known to taste people and then spit them back out again once they realize what they are eating.

The Biggest Party of Them All

Once you've tried your hand in the kitchen, how about hosting an enormous or "Really Big" Party. All you need is

Words to Know

extinct:
When the last of any creature dies, that type of creature becomes *extinct*. To prevent some animals or fish from possible extinction, we have started putting a few of them in preserves, aquariums, protected waters, or zoos.

a few friends to invite. Ask them to wear something that is really big, like a huge hat or shirt, or to bring something big with them. Why don't you and your friends make a gigantic pizza that looks like an open shark's mouth? Its teeth could be triangles of cheese and the tonsils or tongue could be pieces of pepperoni or ham. If you roll the crust in front of the tongue, you can make the edge of the shark's mouth. How about making a really big root beer float for everyone to enjoy with the pizza?

Don't forget to hold a "biggest" contest to see who can take the biggest step or who can make the biggest tower out of cards. Have a competition for the one who brought the biggest thing with them, or you can hold a really big shoe relay. Here's what you need to play this game:

1. Ask if you can borrow a few pairs of shoes from the adults in your house.
2. Draw names for each team, and have each team make two lines facing each other.
3. The first person from each line has to put on a pair of the really big shoes.
4. The person then walks backwards as fast as possible over to his teammates on the other side.
5. When the person reaches the other side, she takes the shoes off and hands them to the next person.
6. Both lines keep going until all the players on one of the teams finish their turns.

Prizes for the winning team could be giant-sized candy bars. The prize for the second place team could be regular-sized ones. Hopefully you will chew your candy bar before you swallow it—not like the sharks, which prefer to swallow their food whole.

What am I?

You might know who I am if you ever "saw" my nose. You may have a tool that looks like me in your toolbox or garage. I am one of the sharpest sharks around. **What am I?**

Sawshark

Fun Fact

Sharks Ahoy!

One reason there have been so many shark sightings reported over the years by fishermen and pirates is because sharks like to follow boats or ships and wait for the food scraps that are sometimes thrown overboard.

Mixed Messages

Some beaches post signs to warn people that swimming could be dangerous.

At this beach, a sneaky shark has moved the letters of the warning sign to make it more to his liking!

See if you can put the mixed-up letters back on the dotted lines where they belong.

HINT: Each out-of-place letter, or pair of letters, is used only once on the correct sign.

_____ ' _____ SWIM
_____ _____ _____ _____
HERE!
SHARKS
ARE N'T
NEAR !
IT IS
SAFE!

thanks!

A HE I N T OT DO

Now That's a Mouthful

It isn't always easy getting along with your family. But can you imagine what it would be like trying to argue with your sister if her mouth was so big it could hold up to six people? Thankfully, you don't have to worry about that—and neither do the sharks, either. The megalodon shark, whose name means "one of tremendous size" and who could also have been known as Big Mouth, has been gone from the oceans for thousands of years. As legend has it, this wondrous fish was so big that at least six men or several sharks could have easily fit into its open mouth. Try to picture yourself swimming along, minding your own business, when this shark as big as a school bus suddenly swims up beside you! If that weren't scary enough, did you know that when objects are seen underwater, they appear to be as big as they really are plus a third of their size on top? So that shark would have looked as big as an eighteen-wheeler!

Water Illusions

Do you want to see how water can magnify something? The next time you are in the bathtub, put your arm under the water and see if looks any bigger than it did before. The water can also make your arms or legs appear to be bent or broken in the place where they start to go under the water. To see this, all you have to do is lie down in a tub filled halfway with water. Have your elbows and knees touch the sides of the tub, while your feet and hands touch the bottom of it. Then look down at your feet and hands. Can you see the strange bend in your arms and legs just where the water hits them? The reason this happens is that light travels through the water at a different speed than it does through the air.

Which One?

I would be a great fish to take along when you go camping. I could be especially handy when you need wood for your fire. Do you know which one I am?

A. Knife fish
B. Spearfish
C. Hatchet fish
D. Razor fish

C. Hatchet fish

What am I?

I have to be one of the most tired sharks around. I'm so tired, I think I could even doze off while I'm swimming up to you.

What am I?

Sleeper shark

Words to Know

spiracle:
A *spiracle* is an opening located above and behind the eye of a shark. This opening acts like a vacuum that pulls water into the shark's gills, allowing the shark to breathe even while it is eating. Not all sharks have spiracles.

Born Swimming

Sharks know how to swim the moment they are born. From the moment they first hit the water, baby sharks—or pups—also know how to hunt for food, eat, and fight.

Another way to see this water illusion is to place a pencil in a clear glass filled halfway with water. Look at the pencil through the glass from the side. What do you see?

Water Ways

Have you ever thought it was strange to have water go up your nose? Just think how confusing it would be to have another set of holes in your head that water could pour into! The angel shark, which hides its body in the sand while it rests, is probably grateful to have a set of spiracles, also known as gill holes, above its eyes. These spiracles allow the water to pour over its gills, so it can take in oxygen and eat at the same time. Most sharks have to decide whether to eat or force water over their gills. You have the same sort of problem when you have to decide if you're going to take a breath or swallow something you ate.

Cold-blooded sharks can go a long time without eating anything. They like to eat every day, just like you do, but they don't *have* to eat for a month. They store food in their liver sort of the way you save money in your piggy bank. The warm-blooded sharks, like the great white and the mako, are the fastest swimmers of the shark family. That's a good thing because the faster they go, the more fish they can catch. Unfortunately, they also have to eat more often because all that swimming around burns up more energy!

Hard to Swallow

Maybe it's because they get too hungry. Or maybe they're just too excited. Whatever the reason, sharks have swallowed some pretty strange stuff over the years—things like nuts and bolts, pieces of wood, clocks, drums, spools of wire, coal, and other items that they couldn't digest. The stomach of a

Alice went swimming and saw a shark, but wasn't scared. Why not?

Answer as many clues below as you can. Write the letters into the grid. Work back and forth between the clues and the grid until you get the answer to the riddle.

1 G	2 C	3 C	4 C	5 H	6 H	7 F		8 B	9 A T
			10 A W	11 D	12 G		13 E			
14 F	15 G	16 B	—	17 D	18 A A	19 D	20 A I	21 E	22 E
		23 G	24 F	25 B	26 B	27 C !			

A. To stand in line
   W A I T
   10 18 20 9

B. Water from the sky
   __ __ __ __
   26 25 8 16

C. Birthday pastry
   __ __ __ __
    3 4 27 2

D. Past tense of eat
   __ __ __
   11 19 17

E. To annoy with scolding
   __ __ __
   21 13 22

F. Bottom edge of a dress
   __ __ __
   24 7 14

G. Lowest man's voice
   __ __ __ __
    1 15 12 23

H. You and me
   __ __
    5 6

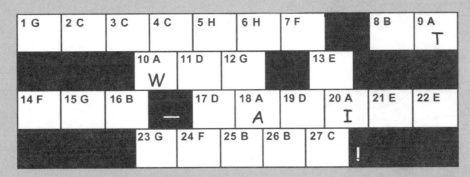

shark can dissolve part of the trash, over a period of time, and the things they can't digest are regurgitated in the same way a horned owl gets rid of theirs. Stories about sharks and whales swallowing humans have been around for years. Have you ever wondered if anyone ever really has been swallowed by a whale or shark and then spit back up again? Were they still alive after they were thrown back out into the water?

Man-Eating Shark?

When you hear someone mention man-eating sharks, almost instantly you feel a shiver go down your spine. But if you were a shark, you would be a lot more afraid of a man eating you! You've probably eaten plenty of fish sticks and fish sandwiches. By this time, you know that sharks are also fish. Did you ever wonder if that fish you were eating was a shark?

When people go to a restaurant, they sometimes like to order shrimp; they might also order crabs, clams, oysters, and lobster. They even eat swordfish, so why shouldn't they eat shark? In other parts of the world, people eat shark soup and shark meat every day. This might sound a little strange until you remember that people also eat turtle, octopus, and raw fish. Shark might actually sound better to you than fish eggs, frog legs, or snails.

Try Something New!

Have you ever dared to try something really new or different? How about one of these combinations: chocolate-covered bananas, peanut-butter-and-cheese-spread sandwiches, or butter and sugar on your pancakes? Someone had to be

Fun Fact

Good Enough to Eat?

Sharks sometimes touch their food before eating it. You probably touch your food before you eat it because you use your hands to put it in your mouth. All a shark really needs to do is open wide and swallow.

the first person to dream up barbecue pizza or create the famous banana split. Maybe you will discover the next new taste sensation. If you think about it, you have probably slowly added many new foods to your diet without even realizing it. You'll never know if you like something unless you try it. Everyone is different. Some people like peanut butter on their eggs, while others eat them with ketchup.

Make a Tuna Boat

Even if you're not interested in eating a shark, you could make yourself a tuna boat. Here are the ingredients you will need:

- 4 buns
- 1 can of tuna (drained)
- 1/3 of a cup of mayonnaise or sandwich spread
- 1 tablespoon of pickle relish
- 2 slices of cheese

All you have to do is mix together the drained tuna, mayo, and relish. Then spread the tuna mixture on one half of the bun and place half of a slice of cheese on top. Ask an adult to broil the tuna boat in the oven for a minute or so until the cheese starts to turn brown. After the adult takes the "boats" out of the oven, let them cool for a minute before you eat them.

Try This

Stress Shark

Use a blue balloon and a funnel made out of paper. Fill the empty balloon about three-fourths of the way full of sand. Stretch the balloon until it's tight and then tie the end of the balloon. Now you can squish your shark into all kinds of shapes or just squeeze it to relieve your stress.

The EVERYTHING KIDS' Sharks Book

How do you make a shark float?

Each of the letters in a column belongs in one of the boxes directly below it. When you have fit all the letters in the proper boxes, the answer will read from left to right, top to bottom.

HINT: The black boxes are the spaces between words.

Letter bank (top grid):

	C	O						A	K				O			
T	C	E			D	A	E	R	P			O			
I	W	O			S	H	O	O	L	S		O	S	D	
O	A	E	E		S	C	S	O	M	A	S	N	D	D	
T	N	K	L		C	R	A	G	D	A	A	A	F	O	F

Answer grid:

T					■		■		L			S	■		
■				D	■		O		■		,		D	■	
	W		■			O				■			■	■	
			■		R		M		■	N		■		
		E				R		!					

> Why can't sharks play tennis?
>
> They keep getting caught in the net!

Chapter 4

Take a Bite out of This!

Say Cheese!

When baby great white sharks are born, they are five feet long, have all their sharp teeth, and are ready to go hunting. They need to be ready because their mothers aren't around to help them find their food. Your family needed to be there to help you after you were born because you didn't have any teeth! Unlike humans, all sharks are born with teeth. Most people get their first tooth before they are a year old. Do you know what the first teeth that you had were called? You guessed it—baby teeth! You didn't get to keep them very long before your second set of teeth started pushing your baby teeth out of your mouth. The same thing happens to sharks. As soon as they lose a tooth, another takes its place. In fact, they have rows of teeth lying down inside their mouth. It's like an escalator of endless teeth!

Bring in the Replacements

Unlike our permanent teeth, which are much bigger than our baby teeth, each of a shark's replacement teeth is just the same as the tooth it just lost. Do you have any pictures of you before you had any teeth? Now take a look at your pictures after you got some baby teeth, and then the ones after your permanent teeth came in. When you compare these pictures, you will see that your smile looks very different. The new teeth are much larger than your baby teeth. There are more of them, and sometimes there isn't enough room in your mouth, which is why some people get braces. Do you know someone who has worn braces on their teeth? Sharks are

Color me in!

What am I?

With my name, you may expect me to have nine lives. But like any other shark, I only have one. I have very different and special feline eyes. **What am I?**

Cat shark

very lucky. They don't keep their teeth long enough to need braces. Can you imagine what a shark would look like with braces? Wouldn't that be scary? How would you like to be a shark dentist and have to adjust those braces?

Making an Impression

When someone needs to have braces, they visit a type of dentist called an orthodontist. The first thing the orthodontist does is make an impression of the teeth, to see which ones will need straightening. To make this impression of the teeth, the orthodontist fills a mold with cold stuff that looks like pink pudding and tells the patient to sink his or her teeth into it.

If you want to make your own impression to see if you have straight teeth, all you have to do is flatten out a spoonful of cookie dough. When you have the dough in a flat circle, place it in your mouth and gently bite down just far enough to see the dents from your teeth. Be careful that you don't bite the dough in half! How do those teeth look?

You can take the rest of the dough and make it into cookies on a cookie sheet and make a different kind of an impression in them with a fork. When you are ready to bake them, ask an adult to put them in the oven for you. After they come out of the oven, you can share them with your family and friends.

Tooth to Tooth

When you checked to see how straight your teeth were, you probably noticed that they had many different shapes. Our teeth come in all shapes and sizes, and many of the shark's teeth are similar to ours.

Your sharp pointy teeth that look like a dog's teeth are called canines, which is another name for a dog. The great

Words to Know

impression:

An *impression* is a mark or dent left behind in an object after something else has been pressed into it. Sharks have left marks or impressions from their teeth in many different things, like surfboards, oars, boats, and even boat propellers.

Which One?

A lot of people might think I can talk, but when I open my beak the only thing that comes out is bubbles. Do you know which one I am?

- A. Cardinal fish
- B. Perch
- C. Parrot fish
- D. Half-beak

C. Parrot fish

Heap of Hammers

Find your way from START to END.

START

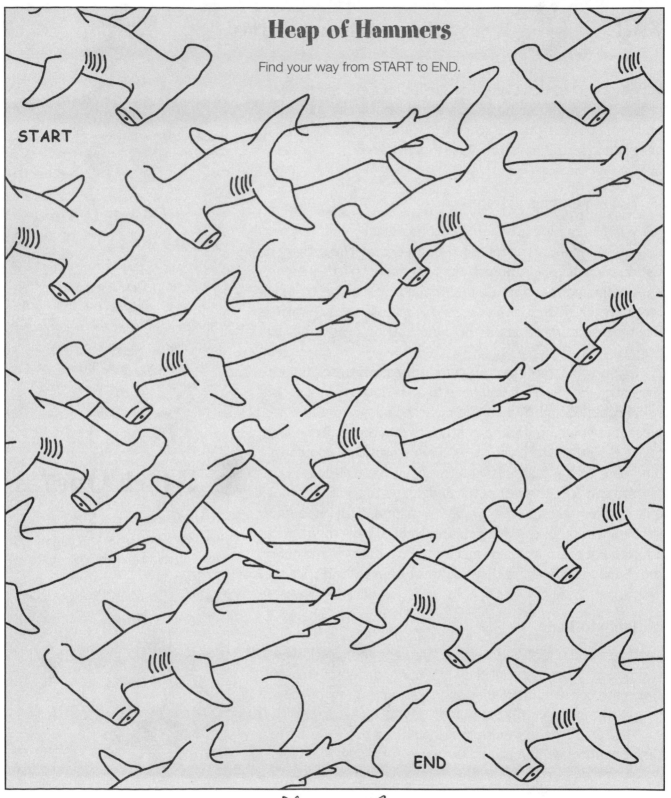

END

white shark also has this kind of teeth. It uses them to tear meat off a bone, just like our ancestors used to do. When people started to eat vegetables, fruits, and nuts, we developed molars to grind up our food. Your molars are the big teeth in the back of your mouth. Sharks like the horn shark that chew up all sorts of animals with shells, like clams and oysters, have molars, too.

Building Supplies

Teeth aren't the only things that can leave an impression. If you press your finger into playdough, it will leave a dent or an impression of your finger. You might even see your fingerprint. You can make your own print, shape your own shark's jaws, or create your own shark teeth with playdough. To make your own dough, all you need are a few things:

- 1 cup flour
- ½ cup salt
- 1 cup water
- 2 teaspoons cream of tartar
- 1 tablespoon cooking oil

Have your parents combine all the ingredients in a saucepan and cook them over low heat until the dough looks like mashed potatoes. Have them pour the dough out onto waxed paper and let it cool for a few minutes. Knead the dough for a short time. This dough dries nicely and stores well in a plastic bag or a plastic tub. If you want your dough to be different colors for the skin of your shark or for the inside of its mouth, you can add contrasting food colors to several sections of the dough.

Which One?

I would jump up and down if it weren't for the fact that I'm always in the water. Do you know which one I am?

A. Orca
B. Sand dollar
C. Man-of-war
D. Frog fish

D. Frog fish

Fun Fact

Cutting Teeth
Most sharks spend their whole lives cutting teeth, thousands of them. Some sharks get a whole new set of teeth as often as twice a month. This means they're cutting a new tooth almost every day.

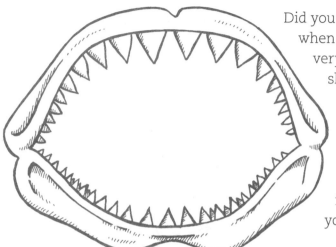

At the Root of It All

Did you ever look really closely at one of your teeth when it fell out? The roots of your baby teeth aren't very long. The roots of a shark's teeth are also short, so they can come out very easily. The tops and sides of teeth are covered with shiny enamel. This enamel is the hardest substance in the body. Turn your tooth over, and look inside. The hole you see is where your tooth was attached to your jaw. Through this opening, your tooth could get what it needed from your body.

The Shark's Mouth

If you've ever wondered what it must look like on the inside of a shark's mouth, you can make a shark's mouth shirt. To make your shirt, you will need the help of an adult, an unwanted white T-shirt, three small plastic bags, three rubber bands, one container of red dye, and a pair of scissors. Then follow these steps:

1. Put the bottom four or five inches of the shirt and the sleeves in a plastic bag (to keep them white).
2. Secure the bag over the cloth tightly with a rubber band.
3. Have your adult helper dip the center of your shirt and the top of the sleeves in the dye.
4. Rinse your shirt until the water is clear and hang it up outside to dry.
5. Cut triangle shapes out of the bottoms of the shirt and sleeves, so they look jagged like teeth.

Going Around in Circles

Sharks spend a lot of time swimming in circles. Do you think they ever get dizzy? Try spinning yourself around in a circle ten times. What happens? Now spin in the other direction ten more times. You can also try spinning in a pool or doing somersaults.

Take a look at some pictures of sharks. What shape would you make those teeth? The makos have teeth like daggers. The goblin sharks are called snaggle-tooths. The tiger shark looks like it truly has saw blades for teeth, and the poor gummy shark looks like it has no teeth at all; all it has are little stubs that resemble flat bricks. (Yes, believe it or not, there is a real live shark called the gummy shark. But you probably wouldn't want to pop him in your mouth!)

Why do these sharks all have such different teeth? One idea is that the shark's teeth have adapted to fit the different types of food that each kind of shark eats, in the same way that human teeth have changed over the years.

Tons of Teeth

Do you know how many teeth you have in your mouth (without looking in the mirror and counting them)? Have you ever wondered if a great white shark would be frightened if he could see himself in the mirror? A great white shark has around 3,000 teeth, but most of them are lying down on the job, waiting until they are needed. A great white shark's teeth can be three inches long! This shark probably loses at least one tooth every day, or around 25,000 teeth in a lifetime. Many of these teeth wash up on beaches, and a lot of people sell these lost teeth for making all kinds of jewelry. There are teeth from all types of sharks. A single tooth can cost as little as a dollar. A megalodon's fossilized tooth, which may be six inches long, can sell for hundreds of dollars.

Hot Stuff

People usually think of sharks as being cool and wet. But that's not always true! Take a red or orange marker and color in all the letters that are not X or Q. When you are finished, read the colored letters from left to right and top to bottom. You will find out how to change a cool shark into some hot stuff!

```
Q H X O X W X Q X C X
X A X Q N X Y O Q X U
X G X E X T X X Q A X X
X Q Q X S X H X A X Q
R X K X Q X T X Q O Q
S X T X A X X R X T A X
X X F Q X I X R X E X X ?
C X H Q X X Q A Q X Q
X N X G X E X T Q X H
E X H X Q X Q I X N X S
H Q X A X Q X R X K X
Q X X T X O X A X P X !
```

 45

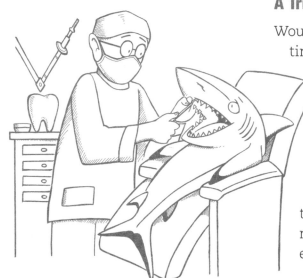

A Trip to the Dentist

Wouldn't it be nice if you didn't have to worry about getting cavities and then having to go to the dentist to have them filled? Some reef sharks have their own kind of private dentist, a cleaner fish called a goby. The goby picks the little pieces of fish out from around the bottom of the shark's teeth. Surprisingly, the goby never seems to be worried that the shark might eat him.

Some animals don't have to worry about their teeth at all because they don't have any! Can you name them? That's right! Birds, turtles, anteaters, and even some whales don't have any teeth.

The Strangest Teeth in the World!

If you think a great white shark's teeth are big, you might be surprised to learn that even its teeth aren't the biggest teeth in the animal world. Do you know that the tusks on an elephant, walrus, or warthog are really big teeth? The beaver's teeth aren't that big, but they never stop growing. By chewing on wood, the beaver keeps its teeth from getting too long. Hamsters have teeth like this, too. If a hamster's teeth kept growing, without getting worn away by chewing, they would eventually grow too long for him to eat with.

Something to Sink Your Teeth Into

Do you, or one of your friends, have a sweet tooth? "Having a sweet tooth" is an expression that means that you like to eat sweet things like candy, cookies, and cake. If you want to please your family or friends, you could mix up a batch of these Garbage Cookies that even a shark would love. To make

Fun Fact

Are You Nosy?
Most sharks have a short and round nose, sometimes called a "blunt" nose. A few exceptions to this rule are the goblin shark, porbeagle, hammerhead, and the common sawshark.

these cookies, all you need is a spoon, a bowl, and the following ingredients:

- 1 cup of margarine
- 1 cup brown sugar (packed)
- ½ cup white sugar
- 1 teaspoon of vanilla
- 2 eggs
- 2 cups of flour
- 1 teaspoon of baking soda
- ½ teaspoon of salt
- ¾ cup of crisp rice cereal
- ¾ cup of potato chips, crushed
- 1 cup of chocolate chips
- 1 cup of candy-coated chocolate pieces
- 1 cup of gummy sharks

Add the ingredients to the bowl in the order they are listed, and mix everything up well. Place spoonfuls of dough on a cookie sheet, then ask an adult to bake these cookies at 375 degrees until they are lightly browned.

Skin, Scales, or Teeth?

Sharks eat all kinds of things, and they live in almost every place in the world. Two body features that they share with their cousins, the rays, are their skeletons and their skin, which is made of little scales that look like teeth.

These scales are called denticles and, like the shark's teeth, they all look different. The denticles vary in size or shape all over the shark's body. The ones on the front edge of their fins look like little knives and help the shark cut through the water easily.

How's Your Balance

Can you balance on one foot? How about on the other one? Can you balance a book on your head and walk? Once you've had some practice, you and your friends can try a balancing relay with plastic bowls of water on your heads. You will want to be outside, where it's okay if you make a mess—and no hands!

Words to Know

denticles:
Sharks have very sharp toothlike scales called *denticles* that cover most of their body. These denticles are also known as the shark's skin.

The denticles along the sides of the shark are designed to allow the water to slip by with very little resistance. Some people think that the sharks can move these denticles so they can swim more efficiently! Do you think that you would want to wear a shark's skin? Swimmers in the Olympics have special swimsuits made like the skin of a shark.

Like Shining Armor

The denticles found on the bottom of the shark are a different type from the ones along the sides. The ones along the bottom are more like the armor that the knights used to wear. This special armor protects the shark from the many dangers lurking below him. Ancient sharks had a similar type of armor all over their bodies. There were other ancient animals that had their own armor too, like shellfish and tribolites. Many animals living today, like the rhinoceros, the armadillo, the porcupine, the iguana, and the alligator, are protected in this way. See how many other animals your friends can name. Do you think that your fingernails could be called a type of armor? An insect's armor, the exoskeleton, is on the outside of its body. Many animals, like the sharks, have skeletons that you can't see. Can you think of an animal that has both an exoskeleton like an insect and an internal skeleton like yours? It's the turtle!

Two Kinds of Skin

Most sharks' skin is no thicker than the heel of your shoe, but the whale shark can have a skin that is almost as thick as a mattress! Its skin is so thick it can stop a harpoon. If the whales, dolphins, and seals had skins like this, it would make it a lot more difficult for the sharks to get their meals.

Try This

A Little Rough

If you look around your house and yard, you will find that several things have a pattern or rough texture like a shark's skin. Some of these textures will appear and make interesting pictures if you place a piece of paper over the item and rub a crayon on the paper. Can your friends guess what the pattern is?

Take a Bite out of This!

The denticles in the shark's skin fall out just like its teeth do. Immediately, a new one pops up to fill the hole in its skin. Do you wish that you had this type of skin when you fall and scrape your knee?

How thick is your skin? Well, it can vary from the thickness of a paper to the rind of an orange. It never gets thicker, because the outer layer falls off. When you take your bath, you can rub off part of this outer layer with a sponge. Our skin also is made up of little building blocks that all fit together.

Fun Fact

A Missing Piece
One common feature of most sharks is what appears to be a cut or notch in their tails. Some of these notches are rather large while others are fairly small.

Hidden Shark

Sneaky sharks like the angel shark are very good at hiding themselves on the sandy ocean floor. There is a sneaky shark hiding in this letter grid, too. Can you find him? There is only one time that the word SHARK is spelled correctly. It can be from side to side, top to bottom, diagonal, or backward!

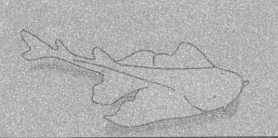

```
S H R K A S H A K A S H
H S H A R S K H A R H A
A S H K A R S K H A R S
K H A R S H A R S K A R
R R K H H S H R K H R S
A K A R K A A K A A S K
H S H R K K R K K H A
R A K R A H A K S S A K
S H R K S K R A H S K A
K A K A R K A K R A R R
H S A R K H K K K R A H
```

The EVERYTHING KIDS' Sharks Book

What am I?

By my name, you might think that I am not the richest shark around. You might also think I am some kind of a dog. **What am I?**

Porbeagle shark

Fun Fact

Seeing Double?

Although sharks are famous for the single dorsal fin most people see sticking up out of the water, most sharks have a second dorsal fin farther down their backs, behind the first.

Rough or Smooth Skin?

Now that you have heard that sharks are covered with teeth, you might have a picture in your mind of a shark with these three-inch-long teeth covering its body! The denticles really don't look like teeth from a distance, though. Even if you could get close enough to a shark to see its skin, you still might not know that the denticles were there unless you touched them. A shark's skin is so sharp you could scrape your hand on it. People have also used shark's skin to smooth wood and metal instead of using sandpaper. But if you stroke the shark's skin in the other direction, it feels smooth.

To get an idea of how this feels, try running your fingers through your hair, starting at your neck moving upward. This works best if you've just had your hair cut short. (If not, try this on someone else who has really short hair.) Your hair, on the upward stroke, would feel like sandpaper. Now try patting your hair back down. Like a shark's skin, it should feel smooth as silk. In fact, there is one shark whose skin feels so smooth that they call it the silky shark, but not all sharkskin feels that smooth!

Some sharks, like the bramble and the prickly dogfish, are covered with spikes that look like spurs or thorns. Other sharks, like the Port Jackson shark, the lantern shark, and the pygmy shark, have enormous denticles right in front of their dorsal fins that look a lot like a big horn or spine.

What do you call a group of 1,000 great white sharks?

Mega-bites!

Chapter 5
Six Senses

To See or Not to See

ave you ever gone on an overnight trip with your family, and then in the middle of the night you woke up and you couldn't figure out where you were? Even at home, familiar things look very different if there is little or no light in your room. See if one of your parents will help you try to travel all over your house in the dark without getting lost. You may find yourself noticing little clues that might tell you where you are, like the breeze from an open window or noise from the street. You might know you are in the living room when you hear the ticking of a clock, or that you are in the kitchen by smelling those chocolate chip cookies that you had for dessert last night.

Do you ever wish that you could see in the dark? Some types of sharks can. But since you can't, you'll have to find your way around with a flashlight. You can play flashlight tag or flashlight hide-and-seek. If you want to have a nighttime scavenger hunt, all you have to do is give everyone a list of items to try to find in the dark and then set a time limit for them to try to find them. When the time is up, see who found the most items on the list. If you live by the seashore, your list could include things like a piece of driftwood, a seashell, a shark egg case, and a lobster claw.

Another fun thing to do is take a night walk to see who else is out in the dark. Some creatures such as cats, raccoons, possums, owls, bats, certain crabs, and lemurs only come out by night.

Try This

Tongue Twisters

Try saying this five times: "Shark-shaped ships are hard to sink, I think." Or try, "Seeing sharks by the seashore certainly is very scary." How about trying to make up a few of your own tongue twisters? Can your friends and family repeat them? Maybe they will make up a few for you to try.

Eye to Eye

The sharks that live below the ocean's surface have a shiny surface within their eyes that can reflect the small amount of light that enters their eyes. So, like a cat, they see well in the dark, and their eyes glow or reflect light. The cat sharks, some of which are also known as shy-eyes, have these kinds of eyes, and when fishermen pull them out into the sunlight, they immediately try to cover their eyes with their tails. Do you think the sunlight hurts their eyes?

Shark Sight

What would the world look like if you could see like a shark? Go outside in the early morning or right before it gets dark. You won't see nearly as many things at night as you do in the daytime; however, this is when the sharks see best. You probably won't see much color, and neither do the sharks.

The great white is one of the few sharks that scientists believe can see in color. Maybe other ocean animals see colors, because they change their skin color or move to areas that match their body color. It would be bad enough not to be able to see in color, but can you imagine what it must be like to have one eye on each side of your head, like a hammer-head shark?

Cover your left eye and then look around. You should be able to see up and down and to the right. Now do the same thing with your right eye. When you are using only one eye, you don't see everything in front of your face. This should give you a good idea of how much a shark can see. If you covered one eye for very long, you would probably get a headache, because your eyes are used to working together. Because their eyes are located on opposite sides of their

What am I?

My favorite place to swim is near shallow waters, harbors, and ports. I carry my babies around in a purse or egg case. You may have seen me in an aquarium.
What am I?

Port Jackson shark

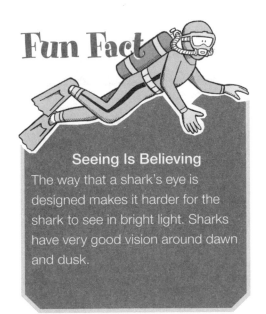

Fun Fact

Seeing Is Believing
The way that a shark's eye is designed makes it harder for the shark to see in bright light. Sharks have very good vision around dawn and dusk.

Which One?

I get teased a lot about my size, just because people think I am really small. But despite my size, I am always a "big" hit on the menu. Do you know which one I am?

A. Minnow
B. Chub
C. Weakfish
D. Shrimp

D. Shrimp

Fun Fact

Eye to Eye

When you compare the eye of a shark to that of a human, you find that they are very similar in a lot of ways. Like your eyes, a shark's eyes have irises, pupils, and lenses.

heads, these sharks can have a problem trying to decide how close they are to their prey, so they have to use their other senses to help them determine that.

Human Sight

How far can you see? An eye test is one way to tell how far you can be from something and still see it. But if you're not at the doctor's office, you can check your eyesight by making an eye chart using different-sized letters of the alphabet. Once you have pasted your letters on a poster-board, have a friend hold the board. Walk twenty paces away, and see if you can read the letters from that distance. If you can't read them, then your partner should slowly work her way in closer to you until you are able to read the letters. Most people have 20/20 vision, which means they can usually see things clearly from twenty feet away. Schools sometimes use a similar test to see if you should have a real eye test done by a doctor. Although trying this activity may give you some idea if you can see things that are very far away, the only way you can know your real score is to have a professional test done in the doctor's office.

Smelling Trouble

Suppose you ask your friend for a drink, and you're thinking that you want water because you are really, really thirsty. Then your friend brings you a glass and you take a big gulp and almost choke on it. What happened? He thought you wanted a soda. Maybe you should have looked at it and smelled it before you took that drink! Has something like that ever happened to you?

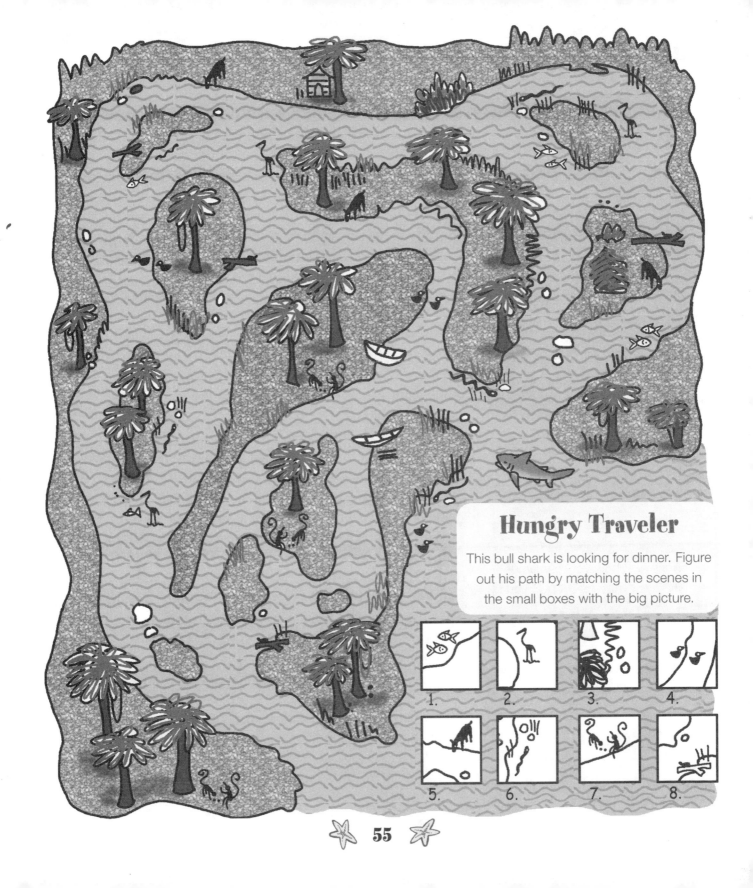

Hungry Traveler

This bull shark is looking for dinner. Figure out his path by matching the scenes in the small boxes with the big picture.

1. 2. 3. 4.
5. 6. 7. 8.

Fun Fact

Do Sharks Have Ears?

You can't see a shark's ears because they are located down inside of the shark's head. Even though you can't see these inner ears, the shark has excellent hearing and balance because of them.

Which One?

Because I am so beautiful, most people think that they would like to touch me. But beware! I can actually sting you with a touch. Do you know which one I am?

A. Rosefish
B. Coral
C. Neon tetra
D. Queen angelfish

B. Coral

Would you know what was in each teaspoon if you had a teaspoon of sugar and a teaspoon of salt in front of you? How could you and your friends tell one from the other?

If you take the wrappers off different kinds of gum, can your friends guess which one is peppermint and which one is spearmint? In each of these examples, you need to rely on your senses of sight and smell before you use your sense of taste to figure out what kind of food is in front of you.

Did You Hear That?

Sharks have many ways to find their food, and they usually are pretty reliable. Scientists believe that the first thing that gets a shark's attention is noise. Sound waves travel really well through water from distances that might be as far as a mile away.

Speaking of sound waves, have you ever blown a dog whistle? A dog hears the high-pitched sound, even though you can't. Sharks hear sounds that are too low for us to hear. Once they hear them, they immediately start to search for whatever made that noise, knowing that it usually means food.

Think of all the sounds that you connect with lunch or supper: sizzling meat in a skillet, the ringing of the timer from a microwave, the noise of a mixer or a blender, or the snap that a toaster makes right before it pops up your bread. What other sounds can you think of that make you think of food?

Nosy Sharks

Talk about a great sense of smell! Scientists believe that a shark can detect blood in the water from farther away than the length of a football field. Once the shark smells blood, it will start swimming in that direction. Although a shark

seems to have a nose like ours, it doesn't have to worry about getting water up its nose or choking, like we do, because the holes in its nose are not very deep. These holes or nostrils are like open bags that allow the water to pass into them and then out again. This way the shark can sample the water and swim towards the strongest smell.

Shocking Sharks

Because sharks have such sharp senses, people may have thought they had superpowers. Have you ever thought that you had superpowers? We do have some senses that are a little hard to explain. Have you ever stared at someone in a crowd, and then they turned and looked at you? Do you sometimes wake up just before your alarm goes off, or can you sense when a storm is coming? Parents tend to know if you are telling the truth or if something is bothering you. They can usually sense when you are in danger, too. Do you believe in ESP (extrasensory perception), the ability to read your friends' minds? Do you say the same thing at exactly the same time that your friends do?

Well, a shark doesn't seem to be able to read minds, but that doesn't stop it from having an edge. The shark uses its ampullae of Lorenzini, which is a big name for a part of its body that acts like a magnet, to sense the electrical charges or radio waves that are sent out by the other animals that are around it. Hospitals and doctors use machines that work in the same way to pick up signals that are coming from your heart and

Try This

Sinking at Sea

If you place an empty cup upright in a sink full of water, the cup will bob and float around in the water like a boat. What does it take to sink it? Try adding a little water in the cup, or maybe add a spoon. Will your cup/boat stay afloat? What if you add even more water?

Soldier Shark

During World War II, there was a very brave kind of shark that went into many battles. These sharks used speed, precision, flexibility, and surprise to score victory after victory.

See what these sharks looked like by following these directions:

1. Find box 1A and copy it into square 1A in the grid.
2. Find box 1B and copy it into square 1B in the grid.
3. Continue doing this until you have copied all the boxes into the grid.

EXTRA FUN: When you are finished with your picture, read more about the amazing "soldier shark" in the answer key on page 130.

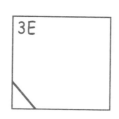
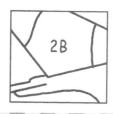
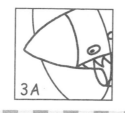

head. Once the shark has found the fish that's sending the signal, he tastes it and quickly swallows it.

Sparks

Electricity is almost everywhere. Sometimes we find it even when we're not looking for it. Maybe you've been shocked when you touched your car door, or when you walked across the carpet and then you touched your television. Static is a type of electricity or charge that can make your hair fly all over the place or your clothes stick to your body. Ask an adult if you can take the socks out of the dryer when it's time to do the laundry. Make sure there are a few fuzzy things in there too, like sweaters and socks. When the dryer's timer goes off, reach in and take out the socks. You may find out that they're already paired up for you. Notice what happens as you try to pull them apart. Do you hear a crackling sound? That sound is static electricity moving from one sock to the other. If you want to see this electricity as well as hear it, take the rest of the socks into a dark room and separate them. What you'll see should look like a miniature lightning storm.

Opposites Attract

Have you ever wondered what it would be like if you never had to look at a map or worry about needing a compass when you went for a walk in the woods? Scientists think that sharks are able to tell where they are by remembering familiar sounds and changes in the flowing water as they travel from place to place. The hammerhead shark is also known for sweeping

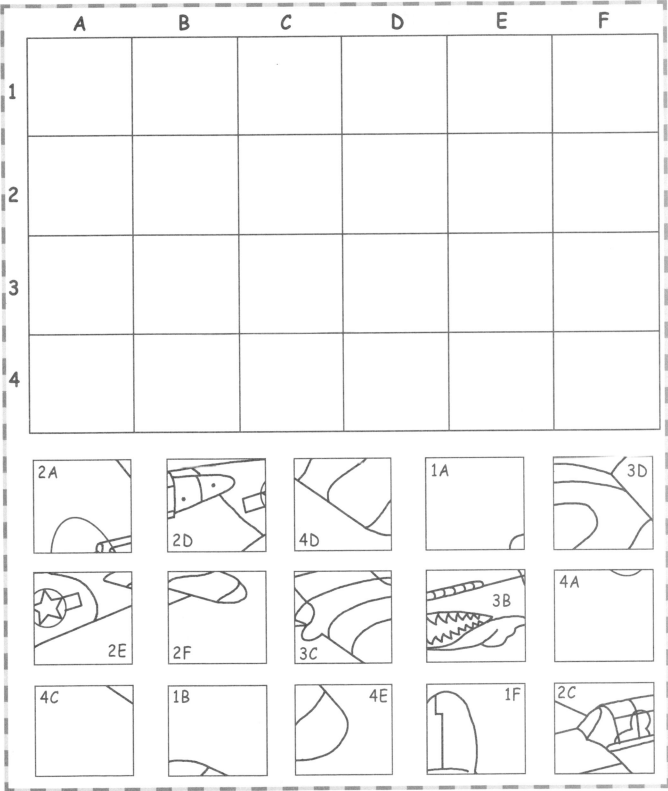

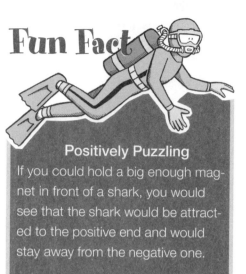

Fun Fact

Positively Puzzling

If you could hold a big enough magnet in front of a shark, you would see that the shark would be attracted to the positive end and would stay away from the negative one.

What am I?

I may look a little strange to you with my eyes and nose on the sides of my head. My shape is the reason I am called what I am. My head looks like I should be hitting nails with it. **What am I?**

Hammerhead shark

the ocean floor with its head and then swimming in a different direction. This makes people wonder if the shark is following the earth's lines of magnetism. They wonder if it might have a type of magnet in its head that it uses like an inner compass.

We do know the earth is an enormous magnet. It would make sense to think that sharks can sense the different magnetic fields, since they can apparently sense electrical charges.

If you want to learn how to make your own magnet, all you have to do is find a large magnet. Then you can make your own magnets by rubbing metal items over the end of the magnet several times. Large magnets with two ends work the best for this. There are several things you can magnetize. A few of them are steel paper clips, iron nails, metal screws, sewing pins, and metal washers.

Headstrong

One of the strangest things about a hammerhead shark is that its head is almost as long as its body. It has an eye and a nostril on either end of its head, and looks more like a silly bathtub toy than a shark. Can you picture what you would look like if you had a nostril and an eye above each ear? The hammerhead is one of the easiest sharks to identify, with its big mouth and skinny body. Because this shark is a killer, you would think that other sharks would avoid it. But fishermen claim they have seen hundreds of hammerheads swimming together in one big school. Maybe these supersensitive sharks somehow know the other hammerheads aren't going to hurt them.

Crossing the Line

Would you like to be able to dodge a ball that was just about to hit you? If you could feel the wind rushing ahead of the ball from several feet away, you could. A shark has a sense called the lateral line that lets it feel movement in the water from many feet away!

Try this experiment with a friend or your family to see what this feels like. Close your eyes and ask the other person to blow through a plastic straw or gently wave a paper fan at different places on your skin. Were you able to decide what object they used and where the air was moving across your body?

If you've ever thrown a pebble in a pond and watched the circles from it move through the water, you have seen the rings of movement or motion. When a fish moves in the water, the shark can feel the same type of waves. Hundreds of sensors make up the shark's lateral line. This line is located on the side of its body. It starts at its head and goes all the way to its tail. Fish that have backbones also have this same type of line. If you look at the side of a goldfish, you can see the line very easily.

A Little Extra Help

Other sharks have another way to find their food. Imagine that you are a hound shark. You have barbels, or strings of tissue, that extend out like fingers so you can touch and sample shallow areas of the ocean floor as you look for food. These barbels send messages to your brain. Now, a shark's brain doesn't look much like that of a human's. The areas of the shark's brain that handle all the information coming in from its senses are much bigger than any other area.

Words to Know

lateral line:
Sharks and fish have a special line, called a *lateral line,* that runs along the sides of their bodies. This line is able to sense movement or vibrations in the water around the shark.

 **Try This**

Magic Magnetic Fish

Make your own magic fish using a paper plate, a picture of a shark or fish with a paperclip attached to it, and a magnet. You can decorate your plate to look like the ocean by painting it or coloring it with markers. Then place your fish on top of the plate and move your magnet underneath, making the fish swim around.

Words to Know

barbel:
The *barbels* on a shark are located under the jaw. These whisker-like feelers sense things in the water, helping the shark to find food.

Find Those Fish!

Have you ever played a game called Marco Polo? It's like playing tag in the swimming pool, only with your eyes shut. It's best to play this game when only the ones who want to play the game are in the pool. It needs to be a very quiet area, so the one who is chosen to be "the shark" can close his eyes and then try to find his "fish friends." When the shark calls out "Marco," the fish have to answer "Polo." They keep moving around the pool to avoid being captured, but usually it is their movements in the water, just like the movements against the real shark's lateral line, that allow them to be caught.

Serious fishermen have machines that almost seem to work like magic. They allow the fishermen to "see" the fish that are swimming hundreds of feet down under the water. The machine produces a signal that bounces off the schools of fish and that lets the fishermen know how many fish are down there and how far away they are. Wouldn't you like a machine like this when it's your turn to be the shark?

Color me in!

Chapter 6
Dynamic Design

Words to Know

anal fin:
A shark's *anal fin* is located on the back of the shark's underbelly. The fin is small but plays a big role in how the shark is able to maneuver around and swim.

Try This

Is it a Bird, a Plane, or . . . ?

Try drawing or tracing the outline of a few different sharks. Now, can you use your pencil to turn their shapes into planes or ships? Try showing your outlines to your family, and see if anyone can guess which outline belongs to which shark. You can give them a list of the sharks' names if they need help.

Streamlined Sharks

Do you ever wonder if the inventors of jet skis, surfboards, submarines, jets, airplanes, and other modern machines got their ideas from looking at these streamlined swimmers, the sharks?

The shark is shaped so that it has points at both ends of its body. This shape is the key to the shark's ability to move through the water so easily. It would be difficult for round-nosed sharks, like the horn shark or megamouth, to move quickly through the water. You might think that the hammerhead shark would have a really hard time. The way it is shaped, the hammerhead may look like it pushes water ahead of itself like a snowplow, but actually the front of its head is turned up like the curved ends of skis. So as long as it is swimming, the water moves upward and over its body. Some sharks move through the water by flexing their muscles from their heads to their tails and swishing their tail from side to side like an eel or a snake. Their dorsal fins work together with their tails to push them through the water.

Dive into This

Since you don't have any fins, you have to pull yourself along through the water by cupping your hands and paddling your feet. When you really need extra speed, you can do the backstroke! By lying on your back and putting your arms over your head, you can pull all the water within your reach towards your body while you kick with your legs. When you do that, you are propelling yourself just like the shark does.

Next time you're in the pool, try floating on your back with your arms close to your sides. The littlest wave and over you go. That's why the shark has pectoral and dorsal fins! Those long, wide pectoral fins of the silky shark,

sandbar shark, and many of the reef sharks are designed to lift the shark up, like the wings of a plane do, and to help the shark turn quickly and steer through the water. The shark uses its fins to balance its body like a tightrope walker.

One type of killer shark that you would never see swimming near your house is called an oceanic whitetip. This shark's scientific name means "longhands," and if you could get one on the X-ray table, you would soon see why. This "longhand" shark's pectoral fins are very long. On an X ray, you might think they look more like a very short man's arm attached to a very big hand.

Have you heard of a real flying fish? These fish like to spend their time swimming around in the ocean, but if another fish starts chasing them, they jump up out of the water, spread their wing-like pectoral fins, and glide through the air, landing somewhere else in the ocean where they'll be safe again.

Color me in!

The Tail End

Not all sharks' tails look alike. The most outstanding tail belongs to the thresher because it is as long as its body. The tail, or caudal fin, helps the shark to swim. The porbeagle, mako, and the great white sharks move more swiftly than other sharks. They have tails that are the same size on top as they are on the bottom. As you learn more about sharks, you may be able to tell what food a shark eats, how fast it can swim, and where it lives just by looking at the shape of its tail.

Words to Know

pectoral fins:
The *pectoral fins* are located towards the front and sides of a shark or fish. They can usually be found under or right behind their gills.

Words to Know

caudal fin:
The *caudal fin* of a shark is the fin located at the end of the tail. Another name used quite often for this fin is the tail fin. The caudal or tail fin on most sharks is larger on the top than the bottom.

What am I?

I am best known for liking to swim really long distances from time to time. I was named for my color that matches the water and the sky. **What am I?**

Blue shark

Have you ever thought about how your legs and feet resemble a shark's tail? Next time you go to the swimming pool, find something to help your upper body float, like a raft or your swim fins, and let your feet move in the water like a shark's tail. Can you get around just by using your "tail"?

The Jawbone's Connected to The?

Many people don't know what to call a shark. Some think that they are mammals like dolphins, humans, or whales. This is probably because a shark's insides, other than its gills, aren't that much different from ours. Others think that sharks are fish because they have fins and gills. The truth is that all sharks are fish, but not all fish are sharks.

What makes a shark different from all the other fish? You could talk about their fins, their scales, their tails, and the way they float in the water, but the biggest difference between most fish and sharks is that sharks have no bones!

The next time your mom or dad opens a can of salmon, look at the bones to see if you can tell what part of the fish they come from. In most fish you can see the vertebrae (or backbone) and ribs.

Bones Versus Cartilage

Have you ever looked at an X ray of your bones at a hospital? If you have, you know that your bones really show up really well, but you can't see the cartilage very well at all. People-doctors have it pretty easy. It's not as easy for a shark-doctor—they have to know if the skeletons in all three hundred and some different kinds of shark are the way they were supposed to be! If you go on the Internet, you can do a search for "X ray human skeleton," and you will get lots of

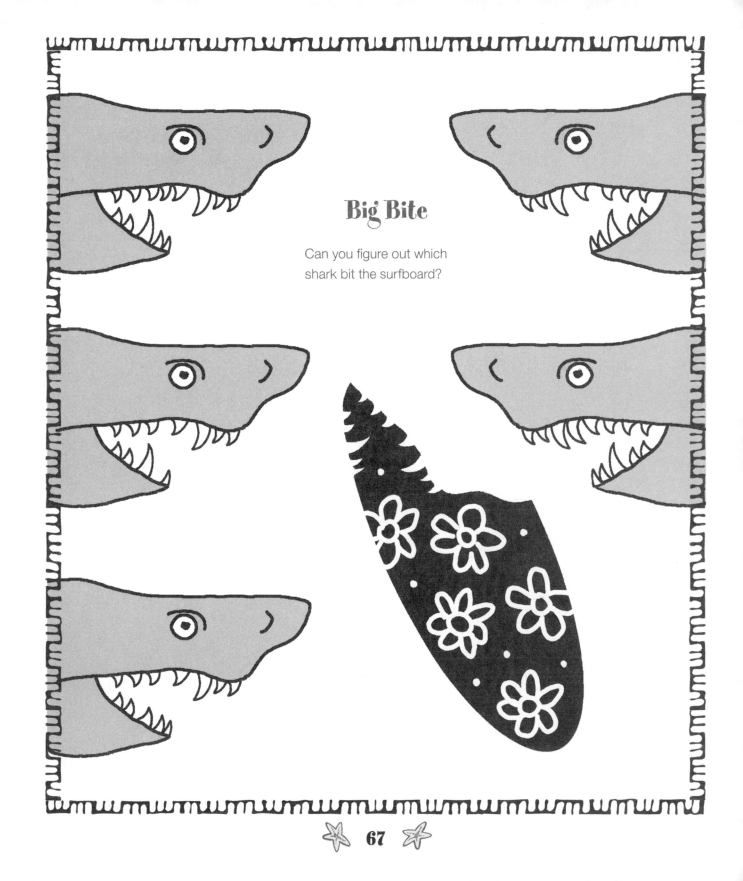

Big Bite

Can you figure out which shark bit the surfboard?

Words to Know

cartilage
A shark's frame is made up of *cartilage* rather than bones. Cartilage is a type of hard tissue—on your body, it can be found in your ears and at the end of your nose.

results that show what your bones look like. Then type in "X ray shark skeleton" to see what the cartilage looks like in a shark's fin. The picture looks more like a ghost skeleton!

The cartilage in your ears feels as soft as a rubber band, but shark cartilage would feel more like the cartilage in your nose. The muscles in a shark's body are what propel it through the water, but because they are pulling on cartilage, instead of bones, the muscles are able to flex more easily. A good example is the leopard shark, which is so flexible that it can squeeze through small holes in coral reefs.

Moving Around

You have immovable joints in your head and partly movable joints in your spine, just like a shark's. Do you think that they have some kind of ball-and-socket joints at the base of their fins like you have in your hips? Can you tell if you or the sharks have a hinge joint in your head? You should know the answer to this the minute you start talking!

Have you ever wondered how some people can wiggle their ears? Some people are double-jointed, which allows them to move their joints in both directions instead of just one. They were probably really surprised the first time one of their joints popped out. They seem to be able to do this trick easily, but very few people have the ability to bend both ways—or maybe it just hasn't happened to them yet!

Counting Bones

Would you like to see what your hand would look like in an X ray? All you need to do is borrow a big flashlight from an adult, turn it on, and hold it under your hand. Then try holding it under your toes to see if it works in the same way. Can you see all the bones well enough to count them? The

number of bones you have has changed since when you were born. No, you didn't lose them. Instead, about fifty of them just grew together.

Have you ever asked yourself, "Why do I need bones?" Well, it wouldn't be much fun lying around on the ground having to worry that you might get squished like a worm, would it? Even a turtle isn't safe inside its hard shell. Tiger sharks have been known to bite turtles in two, shell and all, with their strong teeth and jaws!

Sink or Swim

Airplanes and sharks have two things in common. They have the same shape, and if either one of them stops moving, they start to sink. Most sharks have to keep moving or swimming to get oxygen from the water, but a few sharks have found other ways. The nurse shark has special muscles around its gills that constantly move the water over the gills so that it can stop and rest. The sand tiger shark takes a break by floating, without swimming, never dropping completely to the bottom of the water. To do this, it simply swims to the surface of the ocean, takes a big swallow of air, and then sinks slowly down into the water—over and over again. Probably some of the people who have seen the sand tiger shark doing this have thought they were looking at a whale. Humans have developed many inventions like boats, rafts, and life-vests to make sure that they don't sink in the water. Can you think of other things we use to protect ourselves in the water?

Going Under

Do you sometimes wish that you could breathe under water without a snorkel mask? Let's do some tests to see

Fun Fact

Something to Think About!
If you think that a shark's main concern is food, you may be right. Scientists believe the largest part of a shark's brain is used for smelling. And what could they be smelling? Food, what else?

What am I?

It's as plain as black and white—my stripes, that is. When I am first born, I have dark and light stripes that give me my name. As I grow up, my stripes turn into spots. **What am I?**

Zebra shark

how you and your friends' underwater breathing skills would compare to a shark's:

1. Take a deep breath and see how long you can hold it.
2. Now see how long your friends can hold their breath.
3. Now, measure around your chests. Were the people with the biggest chests the ones who could hold their breath for the longest time?
4. Try measuring your chests before you take a breath and again while each of you is holding it.
5. Compare the measurements. Who took the deepest breath?

When you visit the doctor, ask if you can listen to your lungs with the stethoscope while you're taking a deep breath.

Why didn't the shark buy an electric toothbrush?

Use the tooth decoder to figure out the answer to this riddle. Write the letters on the lines.

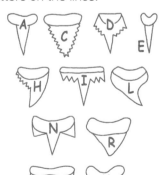

In the ocean, sharks seem to be swallowing water, but actually they are running the water over their gills, which take in water like a sponge. The oxygen in the water travels through the gills, making a trip through the shark's blood and then back out again to be released through the sponge-like gills. This gets rid of the other part of the air that the shark's body doesn't need.

Staying Afloat

Most sharks don't sink because they are constantly on the move. They also have natural buoyancy because the cartilage in their skeleton is much lighter than your bones.

Buoyancy is the quality that determines how well a shark or an object can float in the water. A log will float for a long time until it becomes completely soaked with water, and then it sinks. The first boatbuilders might have seen a log floating down the river and thought that riding, instead of walking, was a better way to travel.

They probably thought it was easier to ride in the log, instead of on top of it, and started to hollow it out. Do you think they kept putting more of their friends into their boat, until it sank? If you were a boat builder, how would you decide how much weight your boats can hold? Ask your parents if you can try a few experiments to see how well things float:

- Try placing a dry sponge in the bath water. Does it float better right away, or after it has been in the water for a while?
- Place several of your toy boats in the water. Why do you think some of them float so much better than the others?
- Put some water in the boats. How much water does it take to sink them?

Words to Know

buoyancy:
When something is said to have *buoyancy,* it means that it is able to float. Some sharks use their buoyancy to rest on the top of the water in the sunshine.

What am I?

I'm the kind of shark you might go down in the swamps to look for. It should be a "snap" for you to guess my name. **What am I?**

Crocodile shark

What's worse than seeing a shark's fin when you are swimming?

Connect the dots from 1 to 73. Then break the number code and fill in the boxes!

19	5	5	9	14	7
8	9	19	8
5	20	8
20	5

Experiments in the Kitchen

Icebergs are just great big ice cubes made from compressed snow, which is basically plain water. So why do they float so well in the salty ocean? If you lived near the Great Salt Lake in the United States, you would see how easy it is to float in its water because it is so salty. Ask your parents if you can use the freezer for a little while to compare how well things float in plain or salty water:

1. Try adding a teaspoon of salt to 1½ cups of water and freeze it in an ice cube tray. Be sure to remember to throw these cubes out after you're done with the experiment!
2. Compare which cubes float best in a glass of plain water: the salt cubes or the ice cubes.
3. Now put a teaspoon of salt in a glass of water and stir it up.
4. Try floating the different types of ice cubes in the salt water. What did you find out?

Try This

Underwater

Have you ever tried to swim down under the water or sit on the bottom of the pool? Your body naturally floats up toward the surface because you have air in your lungs. Try blowing a little air out while you are underwater at the pool or in your tub. Does this help you stay down for a longer period of time?

Floating Treats

Do some frozen liquids float better than others? Try freezing several different types of fruit juices or soft drinks in plastic ice cube trays. Do those cubes float as well in the water as the ice cubes? Now pour some other liquids in glasses and add the juice cubes to them. Do the juice cubes float better in a glass of juice or soda? See if your friends can guess what the original flavors of each of the juices were. Maybe you will have created a new flavor! Keep trying different combinations of liquids and juice cubes until you find one you really like. Ice cream also floats on top

What am I?

With my name, you might expect me to only come out around Halloween. But I make a ghostly appearance all year long. I am known for my scary and ghoulish look. **What am I?**

Goblin shark

Which One?

I may be one of the friendliest and smartest things in the sea. You can see me perform in water shows. Do you know which one I am?

A. Dolphin
B. Killer whale
C. Seal
D. Penguin

A. Dolphin

of soda or fruit juice. Try more buoyancy experiments with banana slices, grapes, cherries, marshmallows, pineapple slices, strawberries, and mandarin oranges.

Is Oil Lighter Than Water?

The biggest fish in the ocean is the whale shark. As heavy as the whale sharks and basking sharks are, both of these huge creatures remain close to the top of the water. That's because the oil in their liver lifts them up to the surface. A bony fish like the goldfish has an air bladder to keep him from sinking. Will an oil-filled balloon float better than one that is filled with water or air? If you want to see if oil really does help the shark float, you will need three small balloons (all the same size), three rubber bands, a small funnel, and some cooking oil.

1. Blow up the first balloon with air. Fasten it with a rubber band.
2. Fill the second balloon with water from your faucet and fasten it, too.
3. For the last balloon, ask an adult to help you pour cooking oil into it, using the funnel. Then fasten it with a tight rubber band.
4. When you are through filling them, put all three balloons in a bathtub half-filled with water.

Which balloon floats the best? Would you rather be the shark filled with oil or a goldfish filled with air? Some kinds of sharks float so well in the water that they can ride the warm currents rising through the water, like a glider does in the air.

Chapter 7
Sizing Them Up

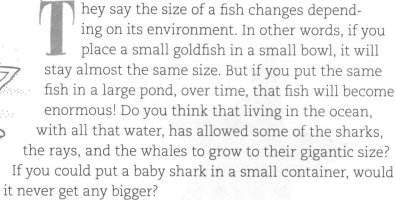

Not-So-Gentle Giants

They say the size of a fish changes depending on its environment. In other words, if you place a small goldfish in a small bowl, it will stay almost the same size. But if you put the same fish in a large pond, over time, that fish will become enormous! Do you think that living in the ocean, with all that water, has allowed some of the sharks, the rays, and the whales to grow to their gigantic size? If you could put a baby shark in a small container, would it never get any bigger?

Basking sharks, the second-biggest fish in the ocean, are as big as a house, with a caudal fin or tail large enough to swat a boat. They got their name because they apparently enjoy basking in the sun. They seem to disappear at certain times of the year. Because some of them have been found without their gill-rakers, scientists think that when they lose these food strainers and can't get any food, they hibernate like a bear until they grow new ones. Can you think of other animals that sleep through the winter?

Was It a Monster?

Several hundred years ago, when a beachcomber stumbled across the remains of a basking shark, he probably thought that he had found a sea serpent. He was sure that this proved that monsters really did exist as they were described in the fairy tales, and he went to tell other people what he had found. When he tried to describe it to his neighbors, they would have laughed and questioned him about how long that creature *really* was.

Can you imagine how the dorsal fins of this mighty shark could look like a sea serpent, especially if a group of basking

Words to Know

hibernation:
Hibernation is a state of being idle or in a deep sleep for a long period of time. It is believed that some sharks, as well as other animals, eat large amounts of food before they hibernate. This food storage helps to sustain them until they become active again.

sharks had been swimming in the ocean? Was this the first fish story?

For years, many fishermen have enjoyed telling tall tales about the huge fish that they supposedly caught, yet somehow this huge fish always gets away. You and your friends could write your own fish stories. Make them as far-fetched as possible: "The fish was so long, it could tie itself in knots," for example. If you look on the Internet and search on the names of different sharks, you could get some good ideas for your stories when you see how strange some of the real-life ocean dwellers really are!

What Do You Believe?

Have you ever heard of Atlantis? Some people believe there are roads leading from the coast of America to this fabled city under the ocean. Others believe that these "roads" are natural stones made from beach rock. Do you believe that the Loch Ness monster is swimming around in a lake in Scotland? Every place in the world seems to have a fish story. The fishermen of the North carved dogfish and other ocean dwellers into their totem poles to bring them good luck, while other fishermen thought they would have bad luck if a thresher shark swam in front of their boat.

Catching a Shark

Greenland sharks are known as sleeper sharks because they like to lie around and sleep. Although they may be almost as long as a minivan and do eat fish, the natives of Canada fear them so little that they catch them using a hook and line. Of course, the line they use isn't lightweight like the fishing line you would use for catching trout.

How Big?

Are you growing as fast as a shark? You can make your own growth chart by gluing several pieces of paper together in a line and marking it like a ruler. Then tape it inside your closet door. Every few months, have someone help you draw a line on the chart to show how much you've grown.

What am I?

If you start seeing spots before your eyes, you might be seeing me. My name sounds more like a creature you would find in a jungle than an ocean. **What am I?**

Leopard shark

Fun Fact

Do You See What I See?

At first glance, a shark's eye may appear to be all black. Actually, their eyes have different-colored irises and white edges around them, just like our eyes.

 Try This

Sticky Sharks

If you want to decorate something with sharks, you can make your own shark stickers or magnets. All you need are a few shark pictures from a magazine. Then you simply glue the pictures to a page of labels or a flat piece of an advertising magnet.

These shark hunters use a rope and a chain to prevent the shark from cutting through the line with its teeth. The only problem with fishing this way is that it could be very hard to cut that chain if the shark turned on you and you wanted to get it off the line.

Do You Have What It Takes?

Throughout history, fishermen have always cared about the number of fish that they catch and how big they were. Think about what you would need if you were going fishing. The most important thing to decide is what fish you want to catch. Then figure out what it would take to catch that kind of fish. For example, you would need a rod and reel if you were going after any small fish, but a really massive rod and reel and a big boat if you're going after swordfish, sailfish, or, of course, shark! You'll also need bait. Some fish, like most of the sharks, will only eat live bait like a smaller fish. What would you put in your tackle box if you wanted to catch a shark?

Contests are held every year to determine who has caught the heaviest or longest fish. Usually, it's better to catch the biggest fish, unless the fish or shark is able to swallow your boat! Imagine the shock of reeling in a shark that big. The sharks that are big enough to swallow a boat are much bigger than land animals, but unlike the land animals, they don't need strong and heavy bones to support their huge size because the water supports most of their weight.

Picture This

When you look at pictures of sharks, what do you see? Does the whale shark, with its stripe-and-dot pattern, make you think of a big sofa with teeth? Maybe the sawshark looks

Ride a Remora

Which remora will get the most points for attaching to this shark?

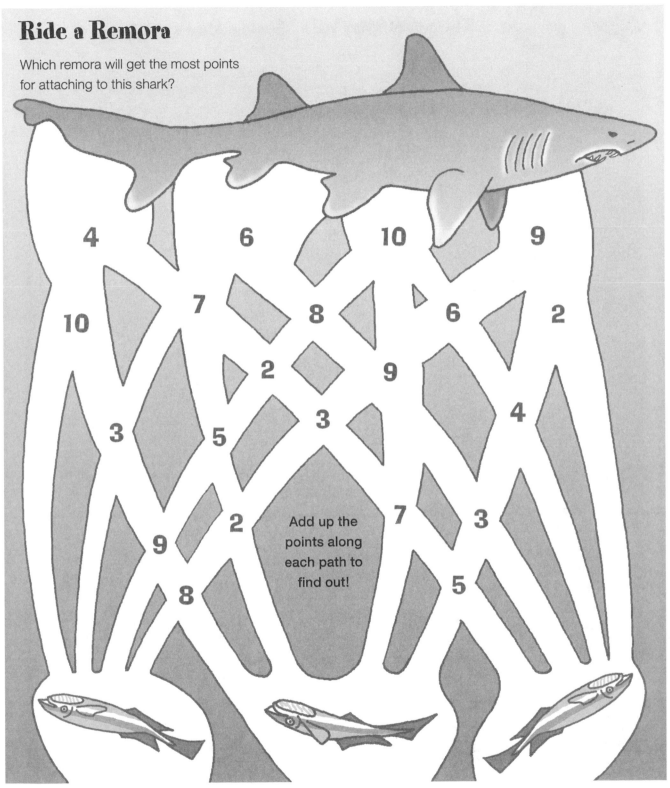

Add up the points along each path to find out!

What am I?

For a shark, there is nothing smooth about me—not even around the edges. If you need a little help I can give you a hint: My name rhymes with "tough." **What am I?**

Rough shark

like a swimming heron with that long beak and beady eyes. The Port Jackson shark looks like it could be related to a dinosaur. See if you and your friends can name some animals that look like sharks or name more sharks that look like animals.

Mysteries in the Ocean

The ocean is so deep that under its surface there are mountains taller than Mount Everest, around six miles high. If you could turn Everest upside down and put it in the Marianas Trench, which is the deepest valley in the ocean, you would still have a mile of ocean above it! Because we haven't seen everything in the deepest part of the ocean, we can only wonder what other kinds of sharks and unusual animals could be living in some of those big holes. Some people believe that there could be an octopus at least 150 feet long, which would be almost as long as half a city block. We know there are tube worms that live in the hot water from volcanoes in the bottom of the ocean, oarfish that look like thin snakes with a red mane on them, and strange-looking ratfish that have no bones in their bodies, just like sharks and rays.

Don't Let Their Size Fool You!

Do you think there is a link between a shark's size and killing ability? Is a big shark always a bad shark? You might think that the huge whale shark would be one of most frightening fish around, but it doesn't even harm the remoras that swim in the ocean with it. If you accidentally reeled one in, you might be afraid that it would swallow you. But like the newly discovered megamouth shark, the whale shark only eats plankton and the small fish that get drawn in with all that water.

Do you think they like to eat these fish? No one knows for sure, but it might be like taking a big sip of lemonade and ending up with the seeds in your mouth!

The great white shark, which usually weighs as much as a small truck and is as long as a small house, is a really big eater. Scientists believe that it eats ten tons of food every year, which maybe isn't that much when you know that the average adult eats the weight of a small car in the same amount of time.

How Do You Rate Them?

Would you think that sharks were the scariest creatures around? Have you ever seen piranhas in the pet store? The piranha is a fish with very sharp teeth that lives in South

Which One?

You might expect to see me shining in the water like a beam from the sun. I am a cousin to the shark. Do you know which one I am?

   A. Brittle star
   B. Barnacles
   C. Ray
   D. Lionfish

C. Ray

Fish Story

Look at these six pictures. Can you number them so that the story makes sense?

Name Game

Some sharks have very descriptive names! See if you can figure out from the small pictures the name of each shark in this puzzle. Write the answers in the numbered grid.

America. They travel together in big groups, looking for food. If an animal enters the rivers where these fish are swimming, it's not very long before there is nothing left of that animal but bones.

The dogfish sharks, like the piranhas, have learned that there is strength in numbers. Their name might make you think that you could pet them like a puppy, but probably the reason that they are called dogfish is because they hunt in packs like dogs. When a bunch of these smaller sharks bands together, they are able to defeat the largest of sea creatures. A pack of sharks can conquer an octopus, which can be as much as 150 times their size. If you were out in the ocean, which one would you rather meet up with, the whale shark or the dogfish?

The odds are better that you would meet up with a dogfish. Their cousin, the spiny dogfish, also known as the spurdog, is the only shark that outnumbers them. At one time, there were so many of these sharks that they were dried and used for firewood! Fishermen disliked these sharks because they ate crabs, lobsters, and also octopus. But if they weren't there to eat the octopus, the octopus would have eaten the crabs and lobsters anyway.

Each animal has a purpose in the food web. The great white shark helps in controlling the numbers of the creatures it eats, but there can't be too many of these sharks or they would starve.

How Big Are They?

Ask your parents if you can make a large mural for the wall to compare the sizes of some of these sharks. There are sites on the Internet (check out the list at the back of this book) or books from the library that will help you find out the sizes of the different kinds of shark. Another way you can

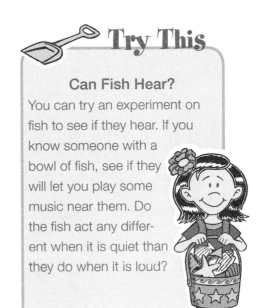

Try This

Can Fish Hear?

You can try an experiment on fish to see if they hear. If you know someone with a bowl of fish, see if they will let you play some music near them. Do the fish act any different when it is quiet than they do when it is loud?

Fun Fact

A Whole Litter

Baby sharks are often called pups. When a mother shark gives birth to her babies, she might have anywhere from one pup to more than 100. Now that's a litter!

Try This

Ocean Toast

To make a piece of ocean toast, all you will need is a piece of white bread, two small cups of milk with two varieties of food coloring in them, and a couple of cotton swabs. Dip the swabs in the colored milk and paint your bread. When you're through, pop it in the toaster, butter it, and eat.

do this is to draw them on the sidewalk with chalk and then let the next rain wash them away. One shark you will have to leave out is the whale shark. If you drew its body to size, it would cover more than a city block, while most of the other sharks could fit on one square of the sidewalk!

A Shark You Could Hold in Your Hand

Sharks come in all different sizes. A baby great white and tiger shark can be about five feet long, but most of the sharks are as small or smaller than you are, even when they're grown up.

You could hold a full-grown pygmy shark in your hand. Think how small their babies must be! These sharks prefer swimming in the waters around Japan, and they travel almost a mile to the surface for food. This would be like you walking ten miles to pick up your lunch! How far would you be willing to swim or walk to find some food?

In the waters near Mexico, you can find another small shark, known as a dwarf dogfish. Is a cigar shark a dogfish? Is a pygmy shark the same thing as a dwarf dogfish? It depends on which book you're reading. With so many sharks that look so much alike, even the scientists and the fishermen don't always know for sure.

What's That Light I See?

The scientists are sure about a couple of things. Almost all the sharks that live far down in the ocean are pretty small, and they use a special light—called bioluminescence—as a way to protect themselves or lure other fish to their mouths. When you're such a small shark, you need something to give you an edge over the other sharks or bony fish.

These sharks usually make the light themselves, or they feed on some other animal that can rub glowing chemicals onto them. Can you name some of these sharks? There are the tiny sharks, like the pygmy shark, the cigar shark, and the cookie-cutter shark. Others are not so small, like the lantern and the megamouth sharks.

Ocean Night Life

If you stand on the beach at night, you may get to see the phosphorescence effect. This is the light that is created when billions of tiny glowing organisms all float in the water. When the water is stirred up by a person swimming or a boat moving through the ocean water, it looks like fireworks! If you want to try to see this, you can ask an adult to take you down to the ocean to watch for it.

You also might see some of the sea creatures that come onto the beach under the cover of darkness to lay their eggs. There might be some new seashells that have washed ashore and hermit crabs that run across the sand like tiny motor homes.

What am I?

Even though I live in the ocean, you might expect to find me in a barn. Just imagine a shark giving milk. **What am I?**

Cow shark

Color me in!

Water World

There are more than 24,000 different species of fish living in the waters of the world! Can you find all the fish swimming in the grid? One has been highlighted for you. When you are done, read the unused letters from left to right and top to bottom to discover just how much of the earth is a water covered habitat.

EXTRA FUN:
Try using a light blue marker or crayon to run a single line of color through each name. It will make the final answer much more interesting!

```
B G P C B A S S A E T S M O R E T H
A S O R O      B K N H S A N T W O T
R S T B A D A I U T O C H I R D S O
R T H I I C P R N L R A F T H E S U
A E U A C E G A E E E T R F A C E O
C T H   D K C S R E O F F T H E E A
U R E A S A L P K A S I R T H I S C
D A N H L T T E A Y S O V E R E D
A U A E L     R B R T H W I T H W A
T R O E W A H O O A C E T E R T H A
K C M A N G L E R U C H T S H O W M
  S M A C K E R E L T K U C H O F T
S T U R G E O N Y W T M H I S P U Z
A H E R R I N G N R E I Z L E I S C
L Y E R P M A L N A L N O V E R E D
M S A R D I N E E S L N W I T H T H
O A H N A R I P L S U O E N A M E S
N G R O U P E R B E M W O F F I S H
```

ABA
ANGLER
BARRACUDA
BASS
BLENNY
CARP
CATFISH
COD
COELACANTHS
EEL
GOBIE
GROUPER
GRUNT
HERRING
LAMPREY
MACKEREL
MINNOW
MULLET
NEHU

OREOS
PERCH
PIKE
PIRANHA
RAY

SALMON
SARDINE
SHAD
SHARK
SKATE

SMELT
SOLE
STICKLEBACK
STURGEON
TETRA

TROUT
TUNA
WAHOO
WRASSE

 86

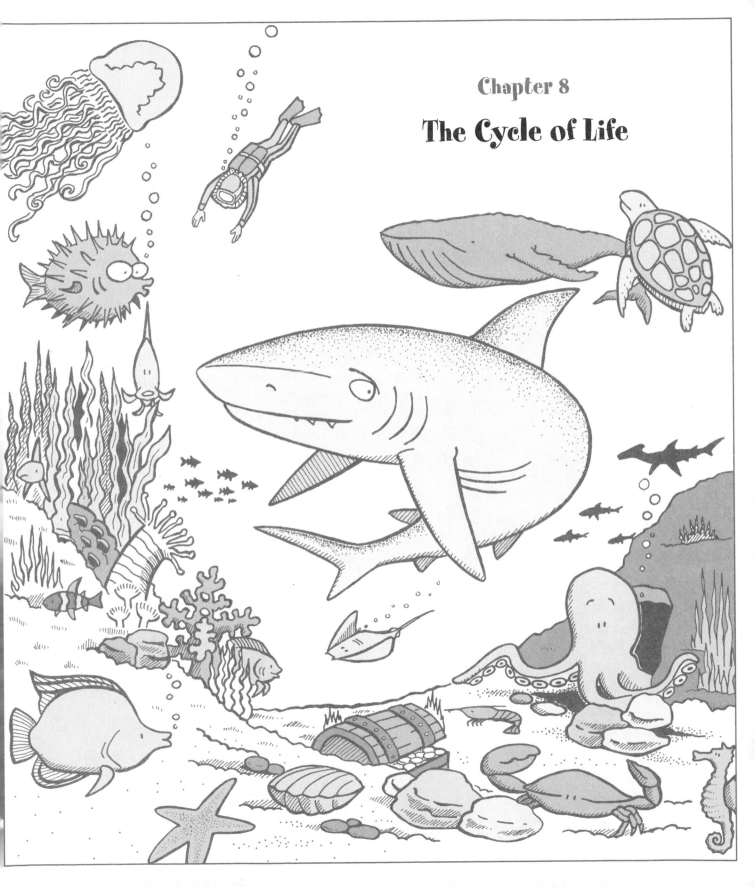

Chapter 8
The Cycle of Life

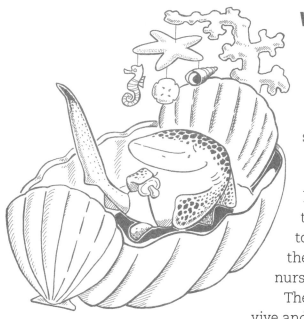

Which Came First, the Shark or the Egg?

Shark eggs can be found in oceans all over the world, waiting for the right moment to hatch. They come in many forms, shapes, and sizes. Depending on what kind of shark they are, some sharks are ready to start their own families less than five years after they are born. Others wait until they are more than twenty years old. Some of the eggs hatch in less than a year, while others can take up to two years—as long as it takes for a baby elephant to be born. When shark babies hatch from their eggs, they don't leave the area where they were born, the nursery, for many months; some don't leave for years.

The baby sharks want to be strong enough to survive and avoid all the dangers lurking outside in the ocean, including the other sharks. What kind of shark would you expect to find in a shark nursery? If you guessed a nurse shark, you're right! Do you know why these sharks are really called nurse sharks? Some say it's because they make a sound when they are eating that sounds like a baby nursing or drinking from a bottle!

Many different types of sharks put their eggs in these nurseries, where there are plants and other hiding places for their babies. One of the favorite spots to have a nursery is in the mouth of a river or bay. Recently, these areas have become more polluted, so they might not be the safest places anymore for baby sharks to emerge from their egg cases.

Some kinds of sharks have at least thirty pups, but others have only one or two. No matter how many pups some sharks have, they can't outnumber the bony fish family. Some of these shark relatives lay millions of eggs at a time.

Fun Fact

New Arrivals

A shark's egg can hatch inside or outside of the mother. Once the egg hatches, the baby shark might be on its own, out in the ocean. Some hatchlings stay inside the mother waiting for the right time to be born, which can take anywhere from a few months to two years. The length of time depends on the type of shark.

The Cycle of Life

If all the animals in the world had millions of babies, where would we put them all? So where do all the millions of bony fish go? Most of them go to lunch with a shark, and only a few return!

Hunting for Eggs

Would you like to have a shark egg hunt? You can make your own shark's eggs by emptying the insides out of eggs that you get from the store. All you will need to make them are some eggs, a drinking straw, a pencil, magic markers or water paints or food coloring mixed in water. Then follow these steps:

1. Poke a small hole in the big end of the egg with a pencil.
2. Move the end of the pencil around until the hole is big enough to fit a straw.
3. Poke another hole in the smaller end of the egg.
4. Now insert the straw in the big end of the egg and blow the egg yolk and white out the other hole.
5. When the shell is empty, you can rinse it out and let it dry.
6. To decorate the eggs, all you need are markers, paints, or food coloring mixed with water in a glass.
7. When you're through decorating your eggs, hide them around the house or back yard. Call your friends or family in to start the search!

If you don't want to hide the eggs that you made, see if you can find some plastic eggs at the store, or use rocks decorated with magic markers.

Words to Know

pollution:

Pollution is the contamination or destruction of any environment, possibly causing harmful side effects for years to come. One type of pollution that may affect sharks is oil spills.

 **Try This**

Do Oil and Water Mix?

When oil is spilled into water, do the two ever mix? Using a clear glass of water, pour two tablespoons of cooking oil in it. What happens? Try stirring the water and oil mixture. What does it look like in an hour, a day, a week? What do you see when you look at the water in the sun?

 89

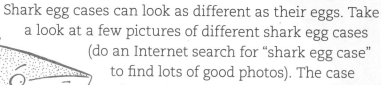

Keep Those Eggs Safe!

Shark egg cases can look as different as their eggs. Take a look at a few pictures of different shark egg cases (do an Internet search for "shark egg case" to find lots of good photos). The case of a swell shark looks like the mother dropped her baby into a basket, and the cat shark's case looks like she placed her eggs into a little bag, which some people have nicknamed a mermaid's purse!

The dogfish shark has the same type of carrier for its babies, but rumor has it that this shark swims around the patches of seaweed with the purse's strings in its mouth until they are tied to a plant.

Making a Mermaid's Purse

If you want to make your own "see-through" pouch or purse, you will need two pieces of soft clear vinyl (like the plastic that is used for photo album pages), and two shoe laces or pieces of yarn or ribbon that are about three feet long. Then follow these steps:

1. Put the plastic sheets together, and use a paper punch to make holes along three sides of the sheets of plastic. Space the holes about one inch apart.
2. Line up the holes and lace up your pouch with the yarn, ribbon, or shoe laces.
3. If you leave a little extra length on the laces, you will have handles for your pouch.

You can fill your mermaid's purse with all sorts of things; be sure to add something special like stickers or gum. After

What am I?

I didn't get my name from honking like a car. It may have been more because I look like a cross between a rhino and a shark. **What am I?**

Horn shark

Why did the shark cross the ocean?

Find your way from START to END. When you have found the correct path, read the letters in order to get the answer to the riddle.

START

END

Which One?

I am thought to be the ancestor of all invertebrates. There isn't too much to me because I am so little. Do you know which one I am?

A. Squid
B. Sea squirt
C. Stingray
D. Scallop

B. Sea squirt

What am I?

Some people believe I am one of the most heavenly sharks you can find in the sea. With my fins shaped like wings, I soar through the water. **What am I?**

Angel shark

you have put a variety of things inside, show them to your friends. Then put the purse away and ask them to make a list of all the things that they can remember seeing inside the purse. At the end of the game, award the stickers or gum to the ones who remembered the most things. You could also pack a snack in the bag when you go on your egg hunts—you could even carry some of your eggs in it.

Cases to See

Carrying a bag on your arm or your back can be hard work, but not as hard as carrying it in your mouth. Horn sharks not only carry their egg cases in their mouths, but they also wind each case into an opening in the rocks on the sea floor. These beautiful polka-dotted egg cases are twisted into a spiral shape that looks like a seashell.

Even if you don't live by an ocean, you can still see some of these cases and eggs—sharks that live in captivity have egg cases, too! The next time you visit an aquarium, ask the guide if any of the sharks currently have egg cases. If you look long enough, you may be able to find them on your own. The cases are usually lying in the bottom of the tank. If they are old enough, sometimes you can see the baby sharks moving around inside them! The same is true for other eggs. If you hold a chicken's egg up to a bright light, you can see inside of it in the same way that you can see inside a shark's egg case.

Making It on Your Own

Once the egg cases are in the ocean, the shark mother goes away. This is probably a good thing, since the hungry mother shark might eat the shark pups. Not all meat-eaters will eat their babies, though. For example, alligators are meat-eaters, too, but they stay with their babies and don't eat them.

Have you ever wondered why some animals care for their babies while others leave them and never see them again? It would be really hard for you to survive if your parents weren't around to teach you to eat, walk, talk, and even swim.

Do you know which of the egg-laying animals act like the shark and which ones act like the alligator? Guess from this list: penguins, lizards, owls, turtles, snakes, and frogs. If you guessed right, you knew that penguins and owls, like most birds, are like the alligator; they build a nest for their eggs and care for them. Some snakes and turtles also stay with their eggs, but frogs and lizards are more like sharks. Some of the shark's relatives, a few kinds of bony fish, carry their babies with them everywhere they go.

Fun Fact

Full Circle
Before a shark eats its food, it will circle it a few times. Have you ever walked around a buffet looking at the food before you try to decide what to eat?

Grandaddy Fish

Write the answers to the questions in the numbered grid. When you are done, the name of a shark will appear in Column A. An amazing fact about this shark will appear in Column B!

HINT:
This rebus puzzle also shows the shark's name.

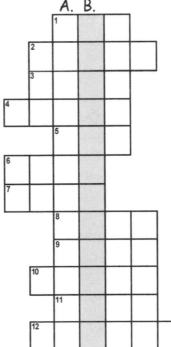

1. Shrewd or crafty
2. Not a knife or fork
3. Close one eye
4. Birds have two
5. Opposite of NO
6. Peas grow in them
7. Owl noise
8. Same as paste
9. Three plus two
10. Bees live in them
11. Opposite of BUY
12. Saying that shows dismay (2 words)

Words to Know

migration:

Migration is the patterned movement of sharks, animals, and other creatures, based on their search for habitat, food, and safety. Several kinds of sharks migrate great distances each year.

 Try This

Do You Migrate?

How about making your own migration map? Maybe your family migrates around town, in your state or country. Decide how big a map you need to cover your journeys. Make a copy of the map, and start drawing different-colored lines for each trip you take. You can also use stickers or pictures to note each place or year.

Sole Survivors

If you have siblings, you know that your brother or sister can really bug you sometimes, but you get over it after a while. Sharks, on the other hand, have been known to eat their brothers and sisters. Does this make your siblings seem a whole lot nicer now? For a shark, it isn't about getting along. It's more about getting a good start in life or just surviving. If there are fewer sharks in the ocean, that means more food for the ones that are left.

Do you ever act like a shark? If you and your friend walked into a candy store and there was only one candy bar left, what would you do? The two of you would probably share it. Now if you were a shark, you might think about having the candy bar as dessert to go with your shark main course. Sharks are not known for sharing or taking turns.

Sharks live to eat and eat to live. No matter whether they are large or small, they have a huge appetite. The first thing a newborn baby shark does is find something to eat!

On the Move

If you were a scientist studying sharks, you would probably notice how sharks follow a pattern of migration, or moving from place to place, the same way birds fly south in the fall and north in the spring.

Have you ever seen ducks or geese flying in a big "V" in the spring or fall? Some people have tracked salmon and found out that they swim for thousands of miles to return to the place where they were born in order to start their own families. All of these patterns of movement are called migration. Scientists believe that these animals have an inborn instinct that makes all this happen.

The scientists have discovered that some sharks, like the blue shark, the mako, and the great white, make very long journeys every year in search of food and to have their young. Some sharks, like the horn shark, don't migrate. They never leave their homes along the shore.

Scientists who want to figure out which sharks travel and where they go have to find a way to track them. How do you think they can tell the sharks apart? It's fairly easy to tell one pet from another. But unlike dogs or cats, many sharks look very similar to each other. So when scientists try to track their migrations, they have to find a way to tag them. Sometimes they will place a tag at the base of the shark's dorsal fin and keep track of the number on the tag. They can also have the shark swallow a transmitter and then let them go. The transmitters send a signal or a type of beep that lets the scientists follow the shark's journey.

Calling All Sharks

You can track your own signal in a game of hide-and-go-beep. All you need is a cordless phone that has a pager button on the base. Test the pager button to be sure it actually beeps the phone. Then you and a friend need to flip a coin to decide who will get to be the first one to hide the phone. The first person hides the phone somewhere in the house for the other person to find. When they are through hiding the phone, they return to the base to press the button. Once the

Color me in!

Which One?

One of my favorite places to float around is in your tub. Some people say I am all wet, but sometimes I'm dry. Do you know which one I am?

A. Seal
B. Narwhal
C. Whale
D. Sponge

D. Sponge

Mermaid's Purses

Look closely at the shark egg cases, or "mermaid's purses," that circle this page. Can you find the comb, mouse, heart, eye, capital letter H, mitten, sock, umbrella, cup, and fish hook that are hiding there?

Now take a close look at these two mermaids and their purses. Can you find the ten differences between them? **HINT:** It doesn't count that they are facing in different directions.

phone starts beeping, see how long it takes the seeker to find it. Now change places and try it again.

How Old Are They?

Every time a new shark comes into the world, it is a new beginning for that shark, but the shark family itself is very old. For millions of years, sharks have survived by following the same cycle of life, just like humans and other animals. They have their babies. The babies grow up, and then they have more babies. Do you know which animal is one of the oldest creatures on Earth? If you guessed the shark, you're right! They're even older than the dinosaurs!

Although the shark family has been around for millions of years, the average shark doesn't live very long. Scientists believe that most of them live only one-fourth as long as humans, but even they don't know for sure.

It's not easy to tell how old a shark is because they are continually losing their denticles and their teeth. Guessing a young shark's age is a lot easier—some baby sharks' spots change, as well as the size and shape of their teeth. Unless you had a baby shark for a pet and watched it grow up, how would you ever be able to guess how old a shark was? The only way we can really know is by keeping track of some of the sharks that are raised in captivity. Some of these sharks have lived in aquariums for twenty years or more.

What am I?

I'm the kind of shark you would expect to find in a circus eating peanuts. When I travel I don't need a suitcase because I have my nose. **What am I?**

Elephant shark

At the Shore

Not all ocean animals live in the deep sea. Many of them can be found at the shore, where the land meets the water. How many of each animal can you find in this picture?

HINT: Some animals are where you might expect to find them, and some are hiding in unexpected places.

crab

scallop

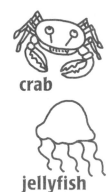

jellyfish

starfish

Chapter 9

Studying the Sharks

Visiting an Aquarium

Have you ever been to a really big aquarium? Most large aquariums are located beside an ocean or a big lake. This gives the aquarium plenty of water to pump into its tanks. The aquariums have special equipment, like big pipes that suck the water up like a giant straw. Then the used water is pumped from the tanks back out into the ocean or lake. Figuring out how to move that much water from place to place took some deep thinking. Probably it also took some experimenting. How far can you move water from one place to another? To make a really long straw or tube, all you need is a package of straws and a friend.

1. Take one straw and squish the end gently until it will fit inside the end of another straw.
2. Slide the first straw a little way into the second one (about half an inch).
3. Add on one straw at a time, and make your pipe as long as you want.
4. When you're done, have your friend place one end of your really long straw into a cup of water.
5. Try to drink the water through your new long straw.

How many straws can you put together and still get a drink?

Who's in There?

The favorite picks for most public aquariums are the nurse and lemon sharks because they are bottom dwellers

Which One?

You might expect to find me in the air, when in fact I am at home in the sea. Do you know which one I am?

A. Sea urchin
B. Porpoise
C. Pilot fish
D. Blowfish

C. Pilot fish

and they don't have to swim to breathe. You can also find black-tip and horn sharks. As aquariums are getting bigger, the variety of sharks continues to increase, too! If you went to Japan, you could visit an aquarium that has a whale shark living in it. Seeing a shark for the first time, especially up close, is amazing. You're fascinated, but grateful that the shark is on the other side of that glass!

Would you expect to see a tiger in an aquarium? You can, but actually it would be a sand tiger shark. Of course, that wasn't always its name. Some people that ran an aquarium changed its name from the sand shark, hoping that the visitors would think that it was a scarier shark!

Bringing Them In

One of the hardest parts of starting an aquarium has to be collecting the sharks. How hard could it be to catch a shark? Because these shark hunters don't want to injure the sharks, they have to catch them with a rope or have them swallow bait. Once the hunters have caught a shark, they have to guide it into a sling so they can transfer it into a tank filled with seawater. It's usually a long trip to the aquarium, so the shark is given medicine to keep it calm and placed in another tank built to let water flow over the shark's head. The water, which is rich in oxygen, helps to keep the shark's insides from drying out while it's not swimming. It is important that a shark's gills and spiracles continually take in water for the shark to remain breathing while it's transferred to its new home.

Other Ways to See Them

Even if you don't live near the ocean or an aquarium, other places like state parks, conservation areas, and pet stores

What am I?

You might think that I am very timid or quiet when I hide my eyes from your view. Really it's the sun that's hurting my eyes. **What am I?**

Shy-eye shark

Fun Fact

Now That's a Mouthful!
Sharks spend most of their time swimming through the water with their mouths open. This is the opposite of humans. We normally like to have our mouths closed and noses plugged when we swim.

 **101**

Fun Fact

Too Salty

The ocean is made up of salt water that contains approximately 35 parts salt to 1,000 parts water. How salty is that? It would be about the same as you adding a half of a teaspoon of salt to your bowl of soup!

often have freshwater fish on display. Some may even have small sharks that you can see. State parks usually have a lot of free information and they often have museums with lots of shells, rocks, or historical artifacts.

Once in a while, sharks and other animals become injured. Injured animals can't go to the hospital. Instead, there are government-operated stations that take injured animals from the Department of Natural Resources, the Coast Guard, or even private individuals who bring them in. They try to return the animals to the wild after caring for them. Some of these places will let you tour their facilities.

Make Your Own Aquarium

If you have ever been to a tropical or salt-water fish store, you've seen the beautiful and bright colors of the ocean. One reason people like to set up their own salt-water aquariums is that they like to see all the strange and unusual ocean life swimming in their own home. You probably won't be able to have a shark in your aquarium, though!

If your parents would rather you didn't have a real fish aquarium, you can still make a dry aquarium as a decoration for your room. You could go to a pet store and buy one of the vase-like containers that are used for betta fish. It should come with a plastic lid for the top. Ask an adult to poke some holes through the plastic with a needle. Cut some black thread to varying lengths. Put fish stickers together, back to back, with the threads between them. Run the thread up through the holes and tie the ends together.

What's the best way to catch a shark?

Answer as many clues below as you can. Fill the letters into the grid. Work back and forth between the clues and the grid until you get the answer to the riddle.

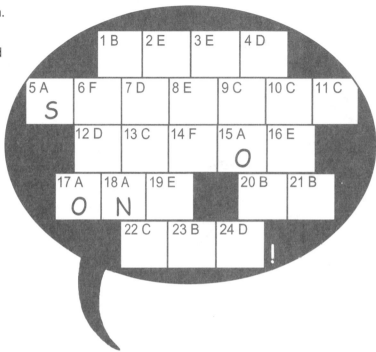

	1 B	2 E	3 E	4 D		
5 A **S**	6 F	7 D	8 E	9 C	10 C	11 C
	12 D	13 C	14 F	15 A **O**	16 E	
17 A **O**	18 A **N**	19 E		20 B	21 B	
	22 C	23 B	24 D **!**			

A. In the near future

$\underline{S}$ $\underline{O}$ $\underline{O}$ $\underline{N}$
5 15 17 18

B. Owl noise

___ ___ ___ ___
1 21 23 20

C. What bees make

___ ___ ___ ___ ___
13 9 10 11 22

D. Not able to speak

___ ___ ___ ___
7 24 12 4

E. To make cloth

___ ___ ___ ___ ___
16 8 2 3 19

F. Word between choices

___ ___
6 14

Words to Know

marine:
Marine life is something that lives in the sea or ocean, like a shark. Freshwater fish would not be considered marine.

What am I?

I would probably be the shark that Snow White would choose for a friend. My size may give you a hint about my name. I like to swim in packs with other fish. **What am I?**

Dwarf dogshark

To Salt, or Not to Salt?

Have you ever gone to the pet store to buy a fish? The first question that they ask is whether you have a salt-water or a freshwater aquarium. This is a very important question. If you have ever looked at your fingers after you've been in the bathtub for a while, you know what the insides of a salt-water fish would be like if you put it in a freshwater tank. If you put a freshwater fish into a salt-water aquarium, its insides would look more like a balloon. A salt-water aquarium is also known as a marine aquarium, because it provides surroundings similar to the ocean.

The ocean has a lot more salt in its water than a lake or stream does. The kidneys of freshwater and salt-water fish have changed, over time, so that different fish are able to live in very different places, like the oceans and the lakes. If you could fit a tiger shark into your home aquarium, it might not need as much salt in its water as some of the other marine animals, because it is able to live where the rivers come into the ocean. A bull shark is the only shark that could live in either type of aquarium, salt or freshwater.

Taking It All In

Of course, sharks need salt water to live. You also need salt in your body. You lose salt from your body when you sweat. In fact, the amount of salt in your sweat and your other body fluids is the same amount of salt that you would find in the ocean. This makes some people believe that it is possible that our ancestors originally came from the ocean water.

Although you don't drink a lot of salt water, you probably eat a lot of salt each day. Most people eat more salt than they should, probably a small bucket of salt a year, but everyone needs to eat some salt because the iodine in that salt helps to prevent disease. For years, man has been trying to figure out how sharks can live so long and seem to be disease free. Do you think all that salt water disinfects and preserves them?

For whatever reason, all animals need and crave salt. Even wild deer will come to a salt block to lick it if you set it out. Salt not only tastes good, but it can also work as toothpaste. If you ever forget to pack your toothpaste or mouthwash, you can brush your teeth with a little bit of salt and then put 1/4 teaspoon of salt in a glass of water and gargle with it.

Fun Fact

Here a Shark, There a Shark
Because different kinds of sharks only live in certain parts of the ocean, you won't ever see all kinds of sharks in the same place at the same time. Some sharks are only found in shallow water, while others only swim where the water is deep.

Scientists and Scuba Divers

Have you ever thought that you would like to live underwater like the sharks? Some scientists lived in an underwater house called Hydrolab. Because they lived there long enough for their bodies to get used to it, they could stay under much deeper water, for longer periods of time. Some lived there for months! Would you like to live underwater and see how sharks live all day and all night long?

Other scientists do not go so deep underwater, and they stay shorter periods of time in vehicles called submersibles. Some of these same vehicles were used to carry divers to and from Hydrolab. Have you ever heard of remote operated vehicles (or ROVs)? These ROVs are unmanned ships hooked to a mother ship that sends them directions on where to go and what to explore. This probably sounds like science fiction, but it's true! Ships of this type were used to explore the *Titanic*. Another submersible vehicle called the *Trieste* traveled down into a place called the Marianas Trench—the deepest spot in the ocean!

There have been many scientists exploring the deep, but no one enjoyed sharing information about the oceans more than Jacques Cousteau, an oceanographer, oceanologist, and

explorer from France. He spent most of his life documenting and filming his experiences in the ocean. With a team of divers and photographers, Mr. Cousteau set out to capture the true world of the shark, one of his favorite subjects.

Who Was in the Cage?

Scientists and scuba divers both know that sharks are quick to bite anything in the water. Because of this, they have learned the hard way that they need to protect themselves by using shark cages. These shark cages could also be called people cages, because the shark is on the outside. Generally the cages are used for studying great white sharks. This is the best way for scientists to learn more about them, since the great white shark won't survive in an aquarium.

Have you ever looked in the eyes of a shark in an aquarium or a gorilla in a cage? Did you ever wonder what they were thinking when they were staring out at those funny-looking humans that are looking in at them?

Working with the Animals

Do you think you would like a job working with animals? Here is a list of just a few of the jobs you could do that involve sharks: marine biologist, aquanaut, oceanographer, scuba diver, divemaster, marine educator, aquatic biologist, hatchery manager, animal trainer, aquarium curator, fisherman, or park officer.

If you decide that you might want to work at an aquarium, you may want to try taking care of a small aquarium. If you don't have one of your own, the best way to do this is to see if you know anyone with an aquarium who will let you help with it.

Words to Know

oceanologist:
An *oceanologist* is a person who studies the oceans and all of the animals, plants, and other things that live in it.

 **Try This**

Writing to an Aquarium
Would you like to learn more about sharks and aquariums? How about writing to an aquarium or zoo that has sharks? When you write your letter, you could ask if they have any information they could send to you. Don't forget to send a self-addressed stamped envelope.

Aquarium keepers have a variety of things to worry about. One of their biggest problems can be figuring out how much to feed a shark. Since sharks tend to gain weight in captivity, the people who run the aquarium sometimes have to put the sharks on a diet or limit their food. Working with sharks can be very exciting and also scary. How would you like to be the diver that feeds those sharks while they are finding out what the right amount of food is for the shark's diet?

Shark Research

Would you even think about trying to pet a shark? The shark has a bad reputation; even its name means villain, like the bad guys in comics or cartoons. Humans really don't understand sharks very well yet. As scientists notice different shark behaviors, they try to figure out why sharks do what they do so we can learn more about them.

How do you feel about sharks? Do you see a shark as a loner, with no friends, simply living to kill? Some scientists believe they like to travel thousands of miles year after year with other sharks. Lemon sharks gather in large groups as though they seem to like being around each other.

Sometimes thresher sharks leap out of the water to turn somersaults for what seems to be sheer pleasure. When other sharks rub against our boats, are they curious about us or are they just trying to get rid of parasites? What shark behaviors are you curious about?

Why do sharks only live in salt water?

The answer to this riddle starts in one of the four corners of the letter grid.
You must figure out which corner, and in which direction the answer reads!

A	W	R	E
T	N	S	P
E	E	S	P
R	E	K	E
M	Z	R	P
A	E	A	E
K	!	H	S
E	S	S	U
B	E	C	A

Words to Know

research:
Many scientists *research* or study different things in the world. Sharks are one thing that researchers would like to study more.

It's Your Turn

Do you want to try a little shark research on your own time? You can learn a lot about sharks on the Internet and in books. If you want to try the Internet, all you have to do is search for the word "shark" in your search engine, like *www.google.com* or *www.yahoo.com*. If you want something more specific, check out some of the Web sites listed in the back of this book. Another way to learn a little more about all kinds of sharks is to visit a library and ask to see their shark books. If you want to go shark watching, ask an adult to take you to the ocean. Take a lunch, binoculars, a camera, a notebook, and a recorder. Researchers sit, watch, and record whatever they see.

Listen to the Lady

Dr. Eugenie Clark knows so much about sharks, her nickname is "The Shark Lady." What does she say about how to behave when swimming in a shark's territory? Color in all the boxes with a dot in the upper right-hand corner to find out!

Chapter 10
The Survival Instinct

Are You a Survivor?

Probably the main reason that the sharks have survived on the planet for as long as they have is that they seem to look out for themselves—and just themselves. Do you have the survival instinct? Have a "Shark Survival" competition. All you need is a few friends and a stopwatch, and the rest is up to you.

Sharks love to be in the water, so for your first competition, each of you will need a pan of water to sit in. The winner of this competition is the person who is able to sit in the water for the longest time. Of course we can't leave out the "Something Fishy Is Going On" puzzle. Everyone gets four shark pictures, cut into three pieces each and stuffed in an envelope. When everyone is ready, open your envelopes and start putting your sharks together. The first person to get all four sharks put together correctly wins.

Another place to hold challenges is in the pool. Everyone can take turns in distance relays for underwater swimming, the crawl stroke, or dog paddling. You could also have a "holding your breath underwater" test or "who can make the biggest splash" competition. You may need a few adults to supervise and judge this part. Don't forget to bring medals or prizes for the winners and treats for everyone who competed.

It Doesn't Have to Be a Competition

Sometimes surviving on your own may mean making your own lunch or entertaining yourself for a few hours. There are several things you can do if you want to spend a little time by yourself: cooking, decorating, drawing, or magic tricks.

Survival Course

How about making an obstacle course for you and your friends? Maybe you have some old tires laying around that you can step through, a few sleeping bags you can do somersaults on, a large box you can crawl through, and so on. For fun, time each other. Can you beat your own time when you practice?

If you want to learn more about cooking, start by looking through a cookbook and ask an adult for help choosing some of the easy recipes. Several recipes do not require any cooking. Foods like sandwiches, salads, dips, and instant-pudding desserts can be made with just a small amount of effort, but they will be sure to make a big impression on your family.

Living in the Ocean

Decorating your room can be as simple as rearranging your furniture or adding a little of the ocean to your private world. Hang some pictures of shells and sharks in your room to give you a sense of being at the sea. You could also see if your family would let you tie-dye a white sheet to make it look like the waves of color in the water. You will need a sheet, at least six strong rubber bands, and a package of blue dye.

1. Roll the sheet up the long way.
2. Wrap rubber bands tightly around the sheet, spacing them three or four inches apart.
3. Have an adult help you place the sheet in the blue dye and let it soak for a little while.
4. Remove the rubber bands. Rinse the sheet in cold water until the water runs clear.

If you take a piece of white tissue paper and place it over a picture of a shark, you can trace the silhouette of the shark. Then you can draw in the additional features like the shark's eyes, mouth, and gills.

If you color these tissue drawings with chalk or colored pencils and tape them to your windows, you will find that they look like stained glass. You can also take several tissue sharks, glue them together in a collage, and put them on a larger piece of paper to make a poster for your room.

What am I?

You might expect me to dislike the color red, or to charge at you when you say "Toro!" **What am I?**

Bull shark

Words to Know

gills:
Sharks have *gills,* which are openings in their sides where water enters their bodies. The gills pull the oxygen out of the water for the shark to use. Once the oxygen is removed, the gills send the water back out again.

Scrimshaw Soap

If you want to try doing your own scrimshaw, all you need is a bar of white soap. On a flat side, draw your shark on the bar using a mechanical pencil. You can add all the borders and designs you like. When you're finished, paint the scrimshaw with dark watercolor paint and wipe the excess paint off.

Where Did It Go?

Another popular hobby is magic. A lot of people would like to be able to make a shark disappear, and now you can! To do this trick all you will need are five plates placed in a row on a table.

1. Place one gummy shark on the first and third plates.
2. Place two sharks on the second, fourth, and fifth plates.
3. Ask your audience how the sharks can be spaced in odd, even, odd, even, and odd order by moving only one plate.
4. When they give up, move the fifth plate over by you and eat one shark (making it disappear) and then slide it back. There should now be odd, even, odd, even, and odd numbers of sharks on the plates.

Be a Card Shark

If you're looking for something else to try, why not become a card shark? When someone is known as a card shark, it means they're so good at cards that you had better watch out! One easy card trick for two people is the "mystery card" game:

1. Before you start your trick, put the card that you need to remember on the bottom of the deck. (Be sure to do this before anyone is watching.)
2. When you are ready to trick your friend, have them pick a card from anywhere in the deck.

3. Once your friend has memorized the card, place it on top of the deck.
4. To show that you're not being tricky, have your friend cut the deck—but only once.
5. Now all you have to do is hold the whole deck in your hands and tell your friend you are going to find the mystery card. To do this, look through the cards until you find *your* card. Your card should always be sitting to the left of the mystery card.
6. Show them the card, and offer to repeat the trick.

You should probably try this by yourself, for practice, the first time.

Things to Do with a Shark

In the ocean, sharks are like living vacuum cleaners! Sharks get rid of dead animals and reduce the numbers of live sharks, so that only the strongest and healthiest survive. Few animals can escape the shark's strong teeth.

Many years ago, people realized that there were many uses for those jagged shark teeth. They saw a better way to cut down a tree and make sharp points for their spears, and they used the delicate blue teeth for jewelry. Have you ever thought about how you could keep your sunglasses on if they had no earpieces? Some people fastened a patch of rough sharkskin to the nosepiece of the glasses and shoved them on their nose! Ouch! Shoes, belts, purses, and billfolds are made from sharkskin. Not only is the leather strong, it is also beautiful. It can be striped, spotted—or, in the case of the whale shark, it could be both!

Fun Fact

Sharks That Really Stick Out
Some sharks make a "point" of not being eaten. These sharks, like the prickly shark, have very sharp denticles that stick out like thorns all over their bodies, making them about as fun to eat as a cactus.

What am I?
You might be able to guess my name if you knew that I love to swallow lots of water until I swell up like a balloon to protect myself from my enemies.
What am I?

Swell shark

Shark Parts

Collect all the words with the same number and write them under the riddle of the same number. Arrange the words correctly to get the answer!

2 cheese!	4 a	3 he	2 the	1 possible!
1 far	2 teeth	4 head	5 pink	5 they
4 tail!	5 if	5 small	1 away	2 are
3 tasted	2 Because	5 shrimp!	3 funny!	4 its
5 and	4 and	1 As	5 would	4 shark's
1 as	2 marks	5 be	2 there	3 Because
4 Between	5 were	2 in	5 Because	5 they

1. What do you get from a bad tempered shark?

_____

2. How can you tell if there's a shark in your refrigerator?

_____

3. Why didn't the great white shark eat the clown?

_____

4. Where is the biggest percentage of sharks found?

_____

5. Why are many sharks big and gray?

_____

Shark Art

Long ago, sailors found a use for another part of the shark. They started to carve pictures into the shark's teeth. Eventually, this type of art came to be known as scrimshaw.

Scrimshaw artists carve pictures into hard surfaces like sharks' teeth and ivory. Once they carve the lines to form their picture, they rub a dark-colored powder over it to make the image show up. When sailors were preparing to work on their shark tooth, what do you think they smoothed it with? Dried sharkskin! This skin, covered with sharp denticles, was called shagreen, and it was used like sandpaper.

Nothing Is Wasted

Other parts of the shark have been used for vitamins; did you ever think that might be one of the things that came from a shark? Researchers think that since sharks seem to be very healthy, they may help us to develop other medicines to cure human diseases. Sharks provide their skin for a variety of uses, the corneas of their eyes for transplants, and oil for the treatment of burns.

Shark meat provides fertilizer and animal feed. Shark parts can also be used to make candles, minerals, and cosmetics, and dried shark can be burned for fuel. People also use sharks for entertainment. How many shark movies have you seen? It didn't take long for man to think of many ways to use his catch. If you were a shark, you wouldn't want to see this list!

Fun Fact

Say AHHH!
If you were to look inside a shark's mouth, you might be surprised to find that a shark has taste buds the same as you do. The sharks use these buds to taste their food so they can decide whether to swallow it or spit it out.

What am I?

By my name, you might expect to find me popping all around the cobbler's bench. Really I'm just one of the longer, skinnier sharks. **What am I?**

Weasel shark

What a Sniffer!

Some sharks have a sense of smell so powerful that they can detect 1 drop of blood mixed into 1,000,000 (1 million) drops of water! Can you figure out how many gallons of water that is? Use the measurements below. You will probably need another piece of paper, a sharp pencil, and a calculator to help deal with the numbers!

60 drops = 1 teaspoon
3 tsp. = 1 tablespoon
2 Tbsp. = 1 fluid ounce
8 oz. = 1 cup
2 cups = 1 pint
2 pints = 1 quart
4 quarts = 1 gallon

ANSWER

SNIFF
SNIFF

Seeing It Both Ways

If someone asked you which animal you like best, the dinosaur or the shark, which would you pick? It's fun to imagine unseen, monstrous creatures lurking in the dark, but it's sometimes easier if that something is no longer a threat to you. Would you want to hug an animal that lives by killing and might hurt you? Well, you probably have stuffed tigers and bears. What are the odds of a shark injuring you? More than a million to one! The odds are greater of your getting hurt by lightning strikes, bee stings, or dogs. But the odds aren't the same of men hurting sharks.

Humans kill millions of sharks every year. Some fishermen believe that sharks are like all the other fish, in an unending supply. If sharks could make movies or write books, they would probably talk about how man threatens their existence!

That's Close Enough!

When you hear people talk about chumming, you probably think they're visiting with their friends. What these people are really doing is delivering snacks to sharks in their own back yard. These shark fans find sharks fascinating and want to be their friends. They feel that if you learn more about the sharks, you'll be more interested in saving them. What they might be teaching them, accidentally, is that man means food, and the beach is the place to go when they're hungry!

There are those who love sharks, and then there are those who don't! If you don't believe in making friends with a shark, would you like to find some

ways to keep them at a distance? Scientists are working on new methods to try to keep sharks away from our beaches and us.

One method that people have come up with to protect themselves from sharks is to stretch a net in front of the beach so sharks can't swim up close to the shore. Scientists are also working on a giant-size version of a device that confuses the sharks' magnetic nose. Another idea is to have other animals around that the sharks don't like, such as killer whales. There is a type of flatfish called the Moses sole fish that may keep sharks away. A shark's jaws won't close on the Moses fish because it can't stand the poison the fish has in its mouth.

Who's the Bad Guy?

Sharks kill to live, but they don't go fishing for man for sport! Some say sharks have been killed in an attempt to make the waters safer for people, but what about safe water for the sharks? Sharks come to their favorite beaches because that's where the best fish are. It's like you going to your favorite restaurant; you pick that restaurant because the food's just better there. Because sharks return to the same places, it is very easy for fishermen to find the sharks. There is one fisherman who claims to have caught thousands of sharks in his lifetime!

Fun Fact

Heads or Tails
Many sharks are named for their color, but some sharks have been named for the shapes of their heads, such as the winghead, scoophead, and the bonnethead shark. Other sharks have been named for the length of their tails.

Which One?

Some may call me grumpy or a kind of hermit just because I like to be alone part of the time. Do you know which one I am?

A. Oyster
B. Crab
C. Conch
D. Limpet

B. Crab

Future Fish

If you could speak for the shark, what would you ask people to do? Every voice, no matter how small, can make a difference. Here are some things people can do to protect the sharks:

- Clean up our shores so the sharks don't lose their babies to pollution.
- Find ways to catch fish so that the fishermen only get the kinds they want.
- Build more aquariums that provide a safe place for sharks to reproduce. By seeing sharks and different kinds of other animals up close, people learn a greater respect for them.

Hungry Shark, Full Shark

Make a path that alternates Hungry Shark (ready to bite) and Full Shark (smiling). You can move up and down or side to side, but not diagonally. If you hit a bitten surfboard, you are going in the wrong direction!

Our future may be related to the world's supply of fish. Fish are one of the foods humans eat, just like beef, chicken, grains, and milk. When you save the fish, it's like saving future fields of grain and herds of cows. Remember, if your food source ever runs out, so do you.

It's the Law!

Grownups try to protect you by making laws that say that you should wear helmets when you ride your bike and wear seat belts when you ride in the car. When your family takes you fishing, there is a limit on how many fish you can catch, so there will be enough fish for everyone. If we make laws that protect all the fish all over the world, then there should always be enough fish for everyone to catch. One reason sharks have survived for millions of years is their home was deep enough in the water to be protected. It has taken a long time to find ways to reach their underwater world.

Now that we have entered their world, we must be very careful not to change it so much that these ancient creatures will vanish forever. Without careful planning, the future of the shark may end up like that of the buffalo and other endangered or extinct animals. Five types of sharks we know of have already become extinct.

Hope for the Future

Like the zoos that have rescued so many of the endangered land animals, aquariums may hold the key to the shark's ultimate survival. Water pollution, increasing temperatures, and overfishing are all threats to the shark's

Try This

Musical Water
Did you know you can make music with water? All you need are a few different sized clear glasses. Fill each one with different amounts of water. To hear the music or sounds the water makes, tap each glass gently on the side with a spoon. Using more or less water will change the pitch of the sound.

Words to Know

endangered species:
An animal becomes known as an *endangered species* if it is in danger of being completely wiped out of existence. Because there are so few of them, the animals become very rare and hard to find.

future. These large fish bowls may provide the safest environment for the shark to exist in until we can solve some of these big problems.

For a long time, people thought the recently discovered bony fish known as the coelacanth had vanished from the earth millions of years ago. Who knows what sharks remain to be discovered in the future, down in the depths of the ocean? Who would have believed a few years ago that eagles, condors, and wolves could be saved? What medical miracle might we discover because we take steps now to save a rare type of shark?

We can help these animals survive if we use what power we have in the right way! Some people write to their U.S. senators or congressional representatives, asking for laws to protect these creatures and the waters that they live in. If you want to learn more ways you can help, or if you're still curious about sharks and other wildlife, tune in to your educational channels. There is new information about animals all the time.

What country is a favorite place for sharks to visit?

Finland!

Appendix A: Glossary

anal fin:

A shark's anal fin is located on the back of the shark's underbelly. The fin is small but plays a big role in how the shark is able to maneuver around and swim.

aquarium:

An aquarium is a container of fresh or salt water where fish and other animals can live. Aquariums can be as small as a fish bowl or as large as a building.

barbel:

The barbel on a shark is located under the jaw. This whisker-like feeler senses things in the water, helping the shark to find food.

buoyancy:

When something is said to have buoyancy, it means that it is able to float. Some sharks use their buoyancy to rest on the top of the water in the sunshine.

camouflage:

Some sharks use camouflage as a way to hide or conceal themselves from others. Their camouflage might be stripes, patches, spots, or colors. The camouflage helps them to blend in with their surroundings.

cartilage:

A shark's frame is made up of cartilage rather than bones. Cartilage is a type of hard tissue—on your body, it can be found in your ears and at the end of your nose.

caudal fin:

The caudal fin of a shark is the fin located at the end of the tail. Another name used quite often for this fin is the tail fin. The caudal or tail fin on most sharks is larger on the top than the bottom.

denticles:

Sharks have very sharp toothlike scales called denticles that cover most of their body. These denticles are also known as the shark's skin.

dorsal fin:

The dorsal fin is the fin that sits on the back of a shark or fish. The size and shape of these fins vary greatly from shark to shark.

endangered species:

An animal becomes known as an endangered species if it is in danger of being completely wiped out of existence. Because there are so few of them, the animals become very rare and hard to find.

evolved:

When something has *evolved*, it means that it has changed. As cats and dogs have evolved, or changed, over many, many years, they have become smaller. Humans have grown taller,

and our brains are getting larger. Some sharks have evolved to allow them to adjust to the changes in their ocean home.

extinct:

When the last of any creature dies, it becomes extinct. To prevent some animals or fish from possible extinction, we have started putting a few of them in preserves, aquariums, protected waters, or zoos.

feeding frenzy:

Sharks have been known to go into what is called a feeding frenzy if they get overly excited when they are hungry and want to eat. In their frenzy, these sharks will even take a bite out of each other.

fossil:

A fossil is a solidified object produced by an organism that has been perfectly preserved in rock or stone. Fossils have taught us a lot about the sharks of the past.

gills:

Sharks have gills, which are openings in their sides where water enters their bodies. The gills pull the oxygen out of the water for the shark to use. Once the oxygen is removed, the gills send the water back out again.

hibernation:

Hibernation is a state of being idle or in a deep sleep for a long period of time. It is believed that some sharks, as well as other animals, eat large amounts of food before they hibernate. This food storage helps to sustain them until they become active again.

impression:

An impression is a mark or dent left behind in an object after something else has been pressed into it. Sharks have left marks or impressions from their teeth in many different things, like surfboards, oars, boats, and even boat propellers.

lateral line:

Sharks and fish have a special line, called a lateral line, that runs along the sides of their body. This line is able to sense movement or vibrations in the water around the shark.

marine:

Marine life is something that lives in the sea or ocean, like a shark. Freshwater fish would not be considered marine.

migration:

Migration is the patterned movement of sharks, animals, and other creatures, based on their search for habitat, food, and safety. Several kinds of sharks migrate great distances each year.

oceanologist:

An oceanologist is a person who studies the oceans and all of the animals, plants, and other things that live in it.

parasite:

A parasite is something that feeds or lives off of something else without giving anything back to its host or food supply. For instance, lice are a parasite that feeds off sharks.

pectoral fins:

The pectoral fins are located toward the front and sides of a shark or fish. They can usually be found under or right behind the gills.

pollution:

Pollution is the contamination or destruction of any ecosystem or environment, possibly causing harmful side effects for years to come. One type of pollution that may affect sharks is oil spills.

research:

Many scientists research or study different things in the world. Sharks are one thing that researchers would like to study more.

spiracle:

A spiracle is an opening located above and behind the eye of a shark that acts like a vacuum that pulls water into the shark's gills, allowing the shark to breathe even while it is eating. Not all sharks have spiracles.

symbiosis:

When two animals help each other, like the shark and the remora, it is called *symbiosis*. Animals or sharks that have learned to live close by each other and work together have this relationship of symbiosis. When they help each other, both can exist.

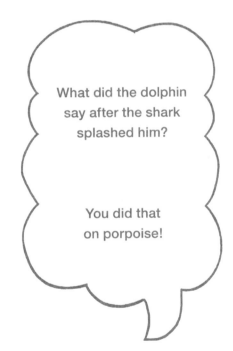

What did the dolphin say after the shark splashed him?

You did that on porpoise!

Appendix B: Do Your Own Research

Books About Sharks

All About Sharks
By Jim Arnosky (illustrator)
Publisher: Scholastic; 1st edition (July 2003)

Chomp: A Book About Sharks
By Melvin Berger (author)
Publisher: Scholastic (March 1999)

Don't Invite a Shark to Dinner (Finding Nemo Stepping Stone)
By R. H. Disney (author)
Publisher: Random House Disney (April 2003)

Draw 50 Sharks, Whales, and Other Sea Creatures
By Lee J. Ames (author)
Publisher: Broadway (May 1991)

Eyewitness: Shark
By Miranda MacQuitty (author), with Dave King and Frank Greenaway (photographers)
Publisher: DK Publishing; 1st edition (June 2000)

Giant Shark: Megalodon, Prehistoric Super Predator
By Caroline Arnold (author), Laurie Caple (illustrator)
Publisher: Houghton Mifflin Co. (August 2000)

The Great Shark Escape (Magic School Bus: Science Chapter Book, Book 7)
By Jennifer Johnston (author), Ted Enik (illustrator)
Publisher: Scholastic; Reissue edition (September 2001)

Great White Sharks (The Untamed World)
By Marie Levine (author)
Publisher: Steck-Vaughn Company (April 1998)

Shark! A Sticker Safari (Discovery Kids)
By Discovery, E P Dutton
Publisher: Dutton Books (October 1999)

Sharks!
By Rhonda Lucas Donald and Kathleen W. Kranking (authors)
Publisher: HarperCollins (May 2001)

Sharks
By Lisa Hilton and Sarah Fecher (authors)
Publisher: Golden Books (June 1999)

Sharks: A Golden Guide from St. Martin's Press
By Andrea Gibson (author)
Publisher: St. Martin's Press (October 2002)

Sharks for Kids (Wildlife for Kids Series)
By Patricia Corrigan (author), John F. McGee (illustrator)
Publisher: NorthWord Press (September 1995)

Sharks: 3-D Thrillers (3-D Books)
By Lynn Gibbons and Chris Coode (authors),
with Meredith Mundy Wasinger and Sarah
Ketchersid (editors)
Publisher: Discovery Kids (June 2000)

Sharks (Zoobooks Series)
By John Bonnett Wexo (author), Barbara Hoopes
(illustrator)
Publisher: Zoobooks/Wildlife Education (February 1998)

Smiley Shark
By Ruth Galloway (illustrator)
Publisher: Tiger Tales (March 2003)

Swimming with Sharks
By Twig C. George (author), Yong Chen (illustrator)
Publisher: HarperCollins Juvenile Books (June 1999)

The Truth About Sharks (Young Readers)
By Carol A. Amato (author), David Wenzel and
Patrick O'Brien (illustrators)
Publisher: Barrons Juveniles (July 1995)

Uncover a Shark
By David George Gordon (author)
Publisher: Silver Dolphin; Book and Access edition (April 2004)

What Do Sharks Eat for Dinner? Questions and Answers About Sharks (Scholastic Question and Answer Series)
By Melvin Berger and Gilda Berger (authors),
John Rice (illustrator)
Publisher: Scholastic Reference (September 2001)

Web Sites About Sharks

Cousteau Society
Join a diving team, play games, or do puzzles.
www.cousteau.org

Discovery Channel: Shark Week
Fun filled site containing 3D sharks, photos,
games, and quizzes.
www.discovery.com

Frequently Asked Shark Questions
When you visit the kids' page, you'll find jokes,
riddles, and strange information.
www.theoceanadventure.com

Monterey Bay Aquarium: Home Page
Watch real sharks swimming around by shark
cam.
www.mbayaq.org

Sea and Sky: Deep Sea Bioluminescence
Board a sub to see the weird and wonderful
world of the sea creatures.
www.seasky.org

SDNHM: Shark Games

Test your shark knowledge using these quizzes, games, and puzzles. You'll find them by clicking the "Fun for Kids" link.

www.sdnhm.org

Shark Anatomy—Enchanted Learning Software

This site is packed with everything you ever wanted to know about sharks, including crafts to make—just click on the "Sharks" link.

www.enchantedlearning.com

Shark Friends

Enjoy a shark theatre, virtual dive, see different sharks' teeth, and more.

www.sharkfriends.com

Sharks

At this site you find shark-filled information, experiments, and lesson plans.

www.oceanofk.org

Sharks and Their Relatives

You find information on this site about the shark's senses, behavior, and characteristics. There is also a good book list.

www.seaworld.org

Where do sharks sleep?

In a waterbed!

What do you get if you cross a shark with a snowman?

Frostbite!

page 5 • Bigger Than Big

Write the name MEGALODON	MEGALODON
Move the G to the beginning	GMEALODON
Move the A to second place	GAMELODON
Move the N to third place	GANMELODO
Move the O to the end	GANMELDOO
Delete MEL	GANDOO
Change D to T	GANTOO
Add I between G and A	GIANTOO
Double the T	GIANTTOO
Add TH to the end	GIANTTOOTH

page 5 • Watch Out!

If you measure the tiny scuba diver, you'll find that you can fit about 11 of him into the length of the shark. That means that this massive Megalodon is approximately 11 times 6, or 66 feet long.

page 7 • Family Reunion

Start with the number of gills you see here...	20
Multiply by the number of eyes the hammerhead has... ②	40
Multiply by the number of dorsal fins on the Port Jackson... ②	80
Subtract the total number of fins on the whaler... ⑥	74
Multiply by the number of pilot fish by the sand shark! ⑤	370

page 10 • Swim with the Sharks

All the answers need the letters "AR". The extra word is "MARK".

1. A dogfish shark does not <u>BARK</u>.
2. Sharks have teeth that are very <u>SHARP</u>.
3. An angel shark does not have a halo or a <u>HARP</u>.
4. The megamouth lives in the deep ocean where it is very <u>DARK</u>.
5. Noah did not bring two sharks into the <u>ARK</u>.
6. You would not find a guitarfish playing music in the <u>PARK</u>.

page 10 • Extra Laps

H	E	N	Y	O	U	C	R	O	S	S	A	S	H	A
W														R
T														K
E														W
G														I
U														T
O														H
Y														A
O														N
D														E
T														L
A														E
H		ANSWER: What do you get when												P
W.		you cross a shark with an elephant?												H
S		Swimming trunks!												A
K	N	U	R	T	G	N	I	M	M	I	W	S	T	N

  127

page 18 • Where's Wobbegong?

page 32 • Mixed Messages

DON'T SWIM
HERE!
SHARKS
ARE IN THE
AREA!
IT IS
NOT SAFE!
thanks!

page 21 • **How Many School Buses Equal One Whale Shark?**

One school bus weighs 5 tons (10,000 divided by 2,000), so one whale shark is equal to three school buses (15 divided by 5).

page 35 • **Alice went swimming and saw a shark, but wasn't scared. Why not?**

1 G	2 C	3 C	4 C	5 H	6 H	7 F		8 B	9 A
B	E	C	A	U	S	E		I	T

10 A	11 D	12 G		13 E
W	A	S		A

14 F	15 G	16 B		17 D	18 A	19 D	20 A	21 E	22 E
M	A	N	—	E	A	T	I	N	G

23 G	24 F	25 B	26 B	27 C
S	H	A	R	K	!

A. To stand in line
W A I T
10 18 20 9

B. Water from the sky
R A I N
26 25 8 16

C. Birthday pastry
C A K E
3 4 27 2

D. Past tense of eat
A T E
11 19 17

E. To annoy with scolding
N A G
21 13 22

F. Bottom edge of a dress
H E M
24 7 14

G. Lowest man's voice
B A S S
1 15 12 23

H. You and me
U S
5 6

page 22 • Let's Play

What's a shark's favorite game?

S W A L L O W
smack, yummy, gulp, urp, urp, slurp, yummy

T H E
yum, crunch, munch

L E A D E R
urp, munch, gulp, gurgle, munch, crack

page 38 • How do you make a shark float?

	C	O			A	K					
T	C	E	D	A	E	R	P			O	
I	W	O		S	H	O	L	S		S	D
O	A	E	E	S	C	S	O	M	A	S	N	D	D
T	N	K	L	C	R	A	G	D	A	A	A	F	O	F

T	A	K	E		A		G	L	A	S	S		O	F
	C	O	L	D		S	O	D	A	,		A	D	D
T	W	O		S	C	O	O	P	S		O	F
I	C	E		C	R	E	A	M		A	N	D
O	N	E		S	H	A	R	K	!

page 42 • Heap of Hammers

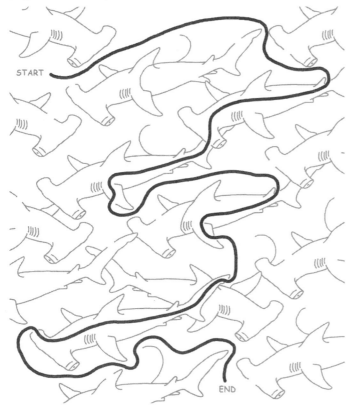

START

END

page 45 • Hot Stuff

QHXOXWXQXCX
XAXQNXYOQXU
XGXEXTXXQAXX
XQQXSXHXAXQ
RXKXQXTXQOQ
SXTXAXXRXTAX
XXFQXIXRXEXX?
CXHQXXQAQXQ
XNXGXEXTQXH
EXHXQXQIXNXS
HQXAXQXRXKX
QXXTXOXAXPX!

ANSWER: How can you get
a shark to start a fire?
Change the H in shark to a P!

page 49 • Hidden Shark

S H R K A S H A K A S H
H S H A R S K H A R H A
A S H K A R S K H A R S
K H A R S H A R S K A R
R R K H H S H R K H R S
A K A R K A A K A A S K
H S H R K K R R K K H A
R A K R A H A K S S A K
S H R K S K R A H S K A
K A K A R K A K R A R R
H S A R K H K K K R A H

page 55 • Hungry Traveler

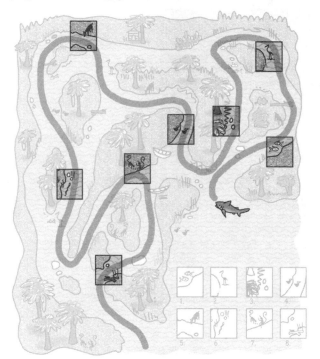

page 67 • Big Bite

page 59 • Soldier Shark

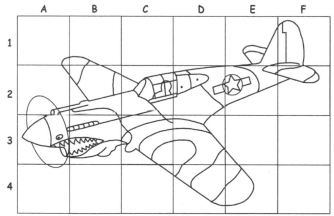

The "Flying Tigers" is another name for the American Volunteer Group who flew during WWII. The front of each Flying Tiger plane was painted to look like a mouthful of sharp teeth—but they were shark teeth, not tiger teeth! Even though their old and battered planes were always short on fuel and parts, the Flying Tigers used speed, surprise, and precision flying to score victory after victory.

page 70 • Why didn't the shark buy an electric toothbrush?

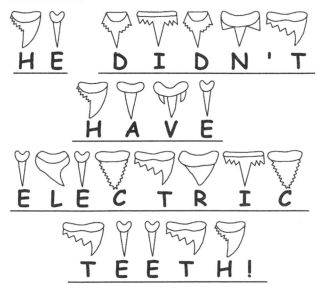

HE DIDN'T
HAVE
ELECTRIC
TEETH!

page 72 • **What's worse than seeing a shark's fin when you are swimming?**

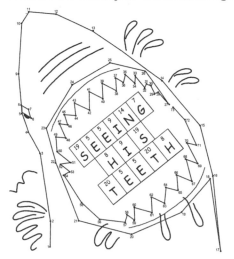

SEEING HIS TEETH

page 79 • **Ride a Remora**

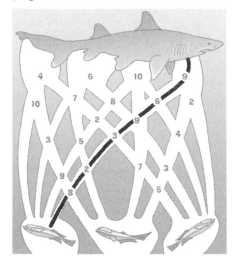

page 81 • **Fish Story**

6 2 5
3 1 4

page 82 • **Name Game**

15. + | 8. | 1.S H A R P N O S E
2.A N G E L | 4.C A T
B U S | T Z
5.C A R P E T | 6.T I G E R
8.W H A L E | 9.B U L L
10.G R E A T W H I T E
11.H O R N
12.C O O K I E C U T T E R
13.H A M M E R H E A D
I
14.D O G F I S H
S
15.S A W F I S H
H

1. | 4. | 5. | 10. (down) +
13. + | 6. | 10. (across) GR8 +
14. + | 11. | 2. | 12.

page 86 • **Water World**

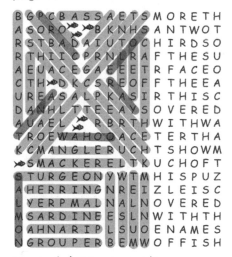

B G P C B A S S A E T S M O R E T H
A S O R O ✦ B K N H S A N T W O T
R S T B A D A I U T O C H I R D S O
R T H I I O P R N L R A F T H E S U
A E U A C E G A E E T R F A C E O
C T H ✦ D K C S R E O F F T H E E A
U R E A S A L P K A S I R T H I S C
D A N H L T T E E A Y S O V E R E D
A U A E L R B R T H W I T H W A
T R O E W A H O O A C E T E R T H A
K C M A N G L E R U C H T S H O W M
✦ S M A C K E R E L T K U C H O F T
S T U R G E O N Y W T M H I S P U Z
A H E R R I N G N R E I Z L E I S C
L V E R P M A L N A L N O V E R E D
M S A R D I N E E S L N W I T H T H
O A H N A R I P L S U O E N A M E S
N G R O U P E R B E M W O F F I S H

Unused letters read:
More than two thirds of the
surface of the earth is covered
with water. That's how much
of this puzzle is covered with
the names of fish!

page 91 • Why did the shark cross the ocean?

ANSWER: To get to the other tide!

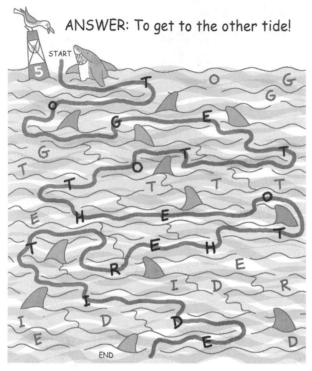

page 96 • Mermaid's Purses

page 93 • Grandaddy Fish

A. B.

1 S	L	Y	
2 S P	O	O	N
3 W I	N	K	
4 W I N G	S		
5 Y	E	S	
6 P O D	S		
7 H O O	T		
8 G	L	U	E
9 F	I	V	E
10 H I V	E	S	
11 S	E	L	L
12 O H D	E	A	R

The spiny dogfish can live to be between 75 and 100 years old!

page 98 • At the Shore

page 103 • What's the best way to catch a shark?

1 B	2 E	3 E	4 D
H	A	V	E

5 A	6 F	7 D	8 E	9 C	10 C	11 C
S	O	M	E	O	N	E

12 D	13 C	14 F	15 A	16 E
T	H	R	O	W

17 A	18 A	19 E		20 B	21 B
O	N	E		T	O

22 C	23 B	24 D
Y	O	U	!

A. In the near future
S O O N
5 15 17 18

B. Owl noise
H O O T
1 21 23 20

C. What bees make
H O N E Y
13 9 10 11 22

D. Not able to speak
M U T E
7 24 12 4

E. To make cloth
W E A V E
16 8 2 3 19

F. Word between choices
O R
6 14

page 107 • Why do sharks only live in salt water?

Answer: Because pepper water makes sharks sneeze!

page 108 • Listen to the Lady

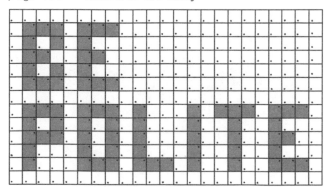

page 114 • Shark Parts

1. What do you get from a bad tempered shark?
   As far away as possible!

2. How can you tell if there's a shark in your refrigerator?
   Because there are teeth marks in the cheese!

3. Why didn't the great white shark eat the clown?
   Because he tasted funny!

4. Where is the biggest percentage of sharks found?
   Between a shark's head and its tail!

5. Why are many sharks big and gray?
   Because if they were small and pink, they would be shrimp!

page 116 • What a Sniffer!

21.7 gallons of water. Here's another way to look at it: a standard bathtub holds about 50 gallons of water when full. So it would only take one teensy tiny little drop of blood in half a bathtub full of water to put some sharks in the mood for food!

page 118 • Hungry Shark, Full Shark

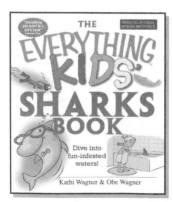
 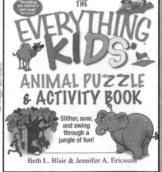